Follow the Directions!

Denise D. Nessel, Ph.D.
Joyce Graham Baltas, Ph.D.

NEW YORK • TORONTO • LONDON • AUCKLAND • SYDNEY
MEXICO CITY • NEW DELHI • HONG KONG • BUENOS AIRES

ICON KEY:

 These exercises complement math curriculum areas.

 These exercises complement language arts curriculum areas.

 These exercises involve science skills, including data collection and observation tasks.

 These exercises involve map skills.

 These exercises are designed for small groups.

 These exercises are designed for partners.

Teachers may photocopy the reproducible pages in the book for classroom use. No other part of this publication may be reproduced in whole or in part, or stored in a retrieval system, or transmitted in any form by any means, electronic, mechanical, photocopy, recording, or otherwise, without written permission of the publisher. For information regarding permission, write to Scholastic Professional Books, 557 Broadway, New York, NY, 10012.

Scholastic, Joyful Learning and associated logos are trademarks and/or registered trademarks of Scholastic Inc.

Home-School Consultant: Susan L. Lingo, Bright Ideas Books™
Cover design by Pamela Simmons and Diana Walters
Interior design by Solutions by Design, Inc.
Interior illustrations by Mike Moran

ISBN 0-439-40813-X

Copyright © 2002 by Denise Nessel and Joyce Baltas

1 2 3 4 5 6 7 8 9 10   40   08 07 06 05 04 03 02 01

TABLE OF CONTENTS

Introduction 4
    From Dependence to Independence 4
    How to Use This Book 4
    How to Be Successful With These Activities 5
    Getting Started 6
    The Ongoing Effort 7
    Checking the Papers 7

Month 1 8

Month 2 11

Month 3 14

Month 4 17

Month 5 26

Month 6 37

Month 7 46

Month 8 54

Month 9 62

Reproducibles 70–80

INTRODUCTION

Almost every teacher has had the experience of giving students clear, detailed directions for completing a task, telling them to get started, and then hearing: "What are we supposed to do?" Most teachers patiently explain again. Some ask those who do understand to explain to those who don't. All can count on repeating the experience, often several times, and wondering in frustration why students can't seem to pay attention. The situation can be just as troublesome when students must read and follow directions on high-stakes tests. Students may take far too long to figure out what to do or may make critical procedural errors and end up with unnecessarily low scores. There isn't a sure-fire solution to this widespread problem, but we've found an approach that works. Most teachers who have tried it have been delighted with how competent their students become at following written directions on their own.

From Dependence to Independence

Most students, eager to please and anxious about doing the wrong thing, have developed deep-seated habits of dependence on teacher guidance and help. Most are accustomed to waiting for the teacher to guide them through activities step by step. Some won't make a move unless a teacher tells them exactly what to do. Others may understand what to do but want frequent reassurance that they're doing it correctly. Of course, teachers do need to give students guidance and help with many tasks, but if teachers are always providing help, they'll simply foster greater and greater dependence.

The first step to helping students with this critical skill is, paradoxically, to stop helping them. Instead the teacher needs to give them directions and let them figure out on their own what to do. This needs to be done regularly and frequently so that students develop habits of independence. At first this may lead to a certain amount of frustration all around because students will get into muddles and express discouragement or give up altogether. Teachers may also feel awkward about not explaining and helping in their usual ways. But gradually students will gain competence and begin to take pride in their growing independence.

The routine is fairly simple: Present one new direction regularly for students to read and follow entirely on their own. These directions are separate from the directions given for regular subject-area activities: They're used solely for developing direction-following skills. As students become more proficient with these special directions, you can have them follow subject-area directions on their own too, so that they're applying their skills directly to homework, quizzes, and various in-class learning activities.

How to Use This Book

We've created 180 directions for you to use with students and have organized them conveniently in monthly sets with suggested goals for each month. The directions are relatively easy at first; they gradually become more challenging. Many are the kinds of tasks students encounter in different subject areas and on high-stakes tests; for instance, there are directions for interpreting maps and charts, using multiple arithmetic operations, and displaying data in various ways.

The variety of tasks here will give students practice responding flexibly to many different kinds of directions. There are activities that involve creating patterns, making up word and arithmetic problems, reading and creating charts, and interpreting and responding to different kinds of information. Some types of activities are repeated several times so that students will have a chance to improve their performance with that type of task. For instance, students are given several opportunities to interpret weather maps and to get information from geographical maps. Of course you may decide to increase the variety even further by modifying these activities to suit your class or by replacing some of them with your own or with activities that students create. Feel free to use this book as a reference point, adapting the activities to suit your needs.

The directions for the first three months are designed for you to give orally. Beginning with Month 4 (page 17) the directions are reproducibles, two or three to a page. Copy these pages, cut on the dotted lines, and store in sequence in a file folder. Note that on some activities there are spaces for the names of the students you choose to collect the papers.

How to Be Successful With These Activities

Teachers are most successful with these activities when they take the time to give a direction every day rather than selecting only a few to use occasionally. Regular, frequent practice helps to develop solid skills and habits of independence. This is especially important at the beginning to get things off to a good start. Then you may want to change the routines a bit (as suggested in the Ongoing Effort section). Here are some other tips for making sure you can help students be successful.

Set short- and long-term goals.
Explain that you want everyone in the class to be able to follow directions independently, without your having to explain anything—including that there are directions to be followed. Tell students that this is the end-of-year goal and that they'll improve from month to month as they perform activities you have planned for them.

Explain why this is important.
Point out that students need to learn to figure some things out on their own, not only because they'll need to do this on tests (when you aren't allowed to help them), but also because the more independent they are, the more competent they'll be with in-school (and out-of-school) endeavors. Invite them to talk about times when it might be important for them to know how to follow directions on their own.

Prepare students for ever-increasing challenges.
Tell students that you'll give them simple directions at first and will gradually increase the challenge as the year goes along. Assure students that they may not always do things perfectly but that only by trying relatively difficult tasks will they increase their abilities. Most important, make sure they know you have confidence in them and that you're sure they'll just get better and better as the year goes along.

Give recognition for effort as well as correct responses.
Since the point of these activities is to build independence, students need praise for the efforts they make to figure things out on their own, even when the work itself falls short. Accuracy will come with time for most children if habits of independence are in place.

Make it fun.
Make posters or banners to raise enthusiasm, and invite students to make new ones periodically. Raise interest and introduce humor by telling students anecdotes from your own experience about the consequences of following (or not following!) directions. Encourage students to recall and discuss times they or their families had amusing experiences with written directions.

Invite reflection and self-evaluation.
At first, have students reflect in small groups or as a whole class on how well they're doing

Follow the Directions! Joyful Learning

from day to day. Encourage children to share their thoughts about their efforts and to trade suggestions that will help everyone be successful. Tell them how you read directions and give them pointers from your own experience. Students who catch on quickly will be good models for the others. Encourage them to talk about how they do what they do. When students discuss their progress, even for just a few minutes every day, they'll start to build a sense of accomplishment as a class, which can inspire everyone to better performance. As students gain skill and are clearly developing independence, you can cut the "debriefings" down to occasional discussions.

Questions That Prompt Reflection

What follows are some questions that we've found to be effective with kids.

- How did you do today with the following-directions activity? Show me by putting your thumbs up for okay and thumbs down if you could have done a better job.
- Which directions were easiest to follow? Why?
- What parts confused you? Why?
- What did you do when you were confused?
- What would you do differently the next time?
- Are there any direction words that you don't understand?
- How can you be sure you have followed the directions correctly?

Getting Started

1. Read the summary and the directions for the first month to get an overview of what students will be doing. A convenient To Do section has tips and suggestions for making things go smoothly.

2. Decide whether or not you want to give students credit for this daily activity, and explain to them what that will involve. Make your expectations clear. You might say something like this by way of introduction:

We're going to start something special that I think you'll enjoy. Every day, I will post some directions here (indicate the place you've selected) that I want you to read and follow. The first directions will be here tomorrow morning. But I won't remind you to do this when we come in tomorrow. I expect you to look here for the directions, read them, figure out what to do, and do it! I'm not going to help anyone because I want you all to learn how to figure things out on your own. I hope you all remember to do this tomorrow because I know you'll be successful!

Once you announce this, it's very important to stick with it. Don't remind students and don't provide help—even if they ask for it! If a student points to the directions and says "What are we supposed to do?" all you need to say is, "Read the directions and do what they say. I'm counting on you to figure them out!" You may even want to print those statements on a note card and show the card to students who ask for help, which will give them a little more practice in reading directions that day.

4. If you have some children who are very poor readers, you may want to set them up with one or more buddies who will read the directions aloud to them each day. In almost all cases, it would be better to provide such help than exclude the poor readers from the activity. Peer help is, in our opinion, better than teacher help in this instance because the poor reader and the buddy are working as a unit to develop independence.

5. Decide on a place in the room for putting up the daily directions. Clear a space on a bulletin

board or the chalkboard, or use a free-standing easel with a flip chart. For the first month, always put the directions in that place so students will know just where to look for the day's activity. As the months go on, you may want to put the directions in different places and make other changes in the routine to keep students interested and to provide new challenges.

6. Be prepared to hear students reminding each other to complete the daily task. It's up to you whether or not you allow this. We tend to think it should be allowed because, in the world outside of school, people remind each other of important things they need to do. In other words, we don't think this should be considered "cheating" because it's a perfectly natural response. You may want to allow this for the first few months and then try to encourage students to be more and more responsible for themselves.

The Ongoing Effort

At the start of each month's activities are suggested goals for that month and a To Do section with tips and suggestions. When you're ready to start that month, skim over the 20 ideas to see if you need to provide anything to accompany the directions (such as a weather map from the local paper). This is also the time to plan which activities you'll use that month and which you want to modify or replace with your own. You're sure to have your own ideas for activities that would be especially good for your students. You may want to jot notes on those ideas in this book for reference throughout the year—and for future years.

You may not want to provide special directions every day. Special events may not allow time for a directions activity, and other schedule changes may make it impossible to get one of these activities in on some days. But if you're as diligent as possible in keeping to the routine, you'll get students into the useful habit of looking for directions to follow as soon as they come into the room. It can be a great warm-up activity, or you may find it's good for settling children down after recess or lunch. Experiment with different times of the day to see what works best for you and the students.

After the first month or two, you may want to vary the schedule in different ways to build in more flexibility and keep interest high. For instance, you could give students an activity every day for two weeks, then take a week off, then every day for two weeks, skip a week again, and so on. Here are some other ways of changing the rhythm once students are comfortable with the process:

- Directions activity on Monday, Wednesday, and Friday, with none on Tuesday or Thursday
- Directions activity on Monday through Thursday, with none on Friday
- Directions activity every day on alternating weeks

Checking the Papers

At first, you'll probably want to check the papers yourself to see how the students are faring and to award points (if you've decided to make this a for-credit activity). At some point you may want to have student teams check the papers for you. Have two or three students on a team, and allow them to work together to go through all the papers. Assign different students to the checking team every few days so that everyone has a chance to take on this responsibility.

We hope you'll find this a useful resource for developing an important skill while having a good time with some very interesting tasks!

Follow the Directions! Joyful Learning

MONTH 1

FOCUS **Students follow directions for completing simple tasks. All but the first tasks involve writing or drawing, and many reinforce such basic skills as correct sentence punctuation.**

TO DO

- Put up a large, colorful DIRECTIONS sign or banner on the chalkboard, a bulletin board, or a flip chart
- Post each day's directions below the sign. At first, remind students *the day before* to look for the directions in that place. Then expect them to remember on their own.
- Place a basket on your desk labeled DIRECTIONS in which students can put their completed activities. From time to time, move this basket to other locations in the room. If students are grouped at tables instead of having individual desks, modify the directions as needed. Suggestions for table use are given in parentheses.

1. Go to your desk, fold your hands, and put a smile on your face. When everyone is seated, ready, and smiling, class will begin.

2. Take out a piece of paper. Put your name in the top right-hand corner. Write a sentence that tells one thing you saw this morning on the way to school. Remember: Sentences start with a capital letter and end with a period. Put your paper in the DIRECTIONS basket on my desk.

3. On a piece of paper, put your name in the top right-hand corner. Write two sentences about a food you like. Remember: Sentences start with a capital letter and end with a period. Put your paper on the right-hand corner of your desk. (Put your papers in the center of the table.) I will collect the papers when everyone is finished.

4. Take out a piece of paper. Write your first name and your last name on the first line. On the second line, write the first six letters of the alphabet. Put your paper in the DIRECTIONS basket on my desk.

5. On the first line of a piece of paper, write your first name and your last name. Skip a line. On the next line, write the numbers from 1 to 8. Put your paper on the left-hand corner of your desk. I will collect your papers.

TEACHER NOTE: Put a stack of note cards on your desk for this activity.

6. Get a note card from my desk. At your seat, write your name on one side. On the other side, write your age. Put your card in the DIRECTIONS basket on my desk.

8

Follow the Directions! Joyful Learning

 7. Take out a piece of paper. Draw two circles, one below the other. Write your first name in the top circle and your last name in the bottom circle. Put your paper on the right-hand corner of your desk. I will collect the papers.

 8. Take out a piece of paper. Draw two circles, one below the other. Write your last name in the top circle and your first name in the bottom circle. Put your paper in the DIRECTIONS basket on my desk.

 **TEACHER NOTE:** Put a stack of note cards on your desk for this activity.

9. Get a note card from my desk. At your seat, draw two circles on the card, one next to the other. In the left circle, write your first and last name. In the other circle, write your age. Pass your card to the person behind you (or next to you). I will collect the cards.

 **TEACHER NOTE:** Put a stack of notecards on your desk for this activity.

10. Get a note card from my desk. Fold it so that the short sides are lined up. Put the folded card on your desk with the fold on the left. Write your name on the front of the card. Put the card on the lower right-hand corner of your desk. I will collect them.

 11. Take out a piece of paper. Fold the paper so that the top edge meets the bottom edge. Inside, on the bottom half, write your name and your age. Put your paper in the DIRECTIONS basket on my desk.

 12. Fold a piece of paper so that the left edge meets the right edge. Inside, on the left side, write your name and your birthday. Put the paper on the upper right-hand corner of your desk. I will collect the papers.

 13. Get out a piece of paper. Place your hand flat on the paper. With a pencil, make an outline of your hand on the paper. Write your name inside the outline of your hand. Put your paper in the DIRECTIONS basket on my desk.

 14. On a piece of paper, draw two circles, one below the other. Write the numbers from 1 to 5 in the top circle and the numbers from 6 to 10 in the bottom circle. Write your name below the bottom circle. When you are finished, bring your paper to me.

Follow the Directions! Joyful Learning

15. Draw two circles, one next to the other. In the left circle, list three kinds of animals. In the other circle, write your name. Turn to the person next to you (or behind you) and share your list of animals. When you are finished, put your paper in the DIRECTIONS basket.

16. Place your hand flat on a piece of paper. With a pencil, make an outline of your hand on the paper. Write a different number inside each finger. Write your name below the drawing of your hand. When you are finished, bring your paper to me.

17. Fold a piece of paper so that the top edge meets the bottom edge. Inside, on the top half, write two of your favorite foods. Write your name inside on the bottom half. Tell the person next to you (behind you) what your favorite foods are, and ask that person to sign your paper underneath your name. When you are finished, put your paper in the DIRECTIONS basket.

18. Fold a piece of paper so that the left edge meets the right edge. Inside, on the right side, write your favorite color. Write your name inside on the left side. When you are finished, tell the person next to you your favorite color and ask that person to sign your paper. Put your paper in the DIRECTIONS basket.

19. On the left side of a piece of paper, write the letter A. Draw an arrow pointing from the letter A to the right. Write the letter B at the point of the arrow. Draw an arrow pointing down from the letter B. Write the letter C at the point of the second arrow. Draw an arrow pointing from the letter C to the left. Write the letter D at the point of the third arrow. Draw an arrow pointing up from the letter D with the point touching the letter A. Put your name at the top of the paper. Put your paper in the DIRECTIONS basket.

TEACHER NOTE: For this activity, CLASS FRIENDSHIP WREATH, each child will need a piece of brightly colored construction paper, a pencil, and scissors. Have these materials on students' desks before they come into the room. You will need to have glue and a large circle of cardboard for students to place their hand cutouts on.

20. Place your hand flat on the piece of construction paper. With a pencil, outline your hand on the paper. Cut out the outline of your hand. Bring your cutout up to my desk. Be ready to put glue on your cutout and put it on our Class Friendship Wreath.

MONTH 2

FOCUS   Students continue with simple directions for paper-and-pencil tasks. Additional challenges include frequent use of typical direction words such as "circle" and "underline" and variations in the way the directions are posted.

TO DO

- Leave the DIRECTIONS sign or banner in the original place, and put a second one in another place such as a cabinet or closet door, an easel, or sturdy poster board hanging from the ceiling.
- Tell students that the directions will be posted each day in one of those two places and that it is their responsibility to find and follow them at the usual time.
- Also tell them you'll be moving the DIRECTIONS basket from time to time and that they'll have to look for it themselves.
- Put the basket in a different place every few days.

1. On a piece of notebook paper, draw a circle near the top of the page. Print your first name inside the circle. Below the circle, print two interesting words that start with the first letter of your name. Find the DIRECTIONS basket and put your paper there.

TEACHER NOTE: Put a stack of note cards on your desk for this activity.

2. Get a note card from my desk. Write the word CALL at the top of the card. Underneath that word, write five words that rhyme with call. Put your name on the other side of the card and underline it. Fold your card in half and put it in the DIRECTIONS basket.

3. Use a piece of lined paper for this activity. Print your name down the left side of the paper by putting one letter on each line. For each letter, think of a word that starts with that letter and that describes you. Write one word on each line, using each letter of your name as the first letter of a word. Leave your paper on the upper right-hand side of your desk. _____ (insert a student's name) will collect the papers and bring them to me.

4. Find something in the room that has a square shape. Draw a picture of it, and write the name of the thing underneath your drawing. Put your name at the top of your paper in the left-hand corner. Turn to the person next to you (or behind you) and share your picture. Have that person sign your paper. Find the DIRECTIONS basket and put your paper in it.

5. On a piece of lined paper, print your name down the left side of the page by putting one letter on each line. Circle each letter. Then, for each letter, think of a kind of animal that starts with that letter. Write the animal names on the lines, using the letters of your name as the first letters. Fold your paper in half. Find the DIRECTIONS basket and put your paper in it.

Follow the Directions! Joyful Learning   11

6. Look around the room at the different colors people are wearing. Count the number of people wearing something green. Write the number on a piece of paper. Put your name on the paper in the upper right-hand corner. Show your answer to a person sitting near you, then write that person's name on your paper. When you are finished, bring your paper to me.

7. Find an example of something in the room that is shaped like a circle. Write a sentence to tell what you found. Write your name underneath the sentence, and draw a circle around your name. Put your paper in the DIRECTIONS basket.

8. Look around the room at the different colors people are wearing. Count the number of girls wearing something red and the number of boys wearing something red. Write a sentence to report your findings. Print your name underneath your sentence. Come up to my desk and read your sentence to me.

9. Draw a circle on a piece of notebook paper. Draw a triangle inside the circle so that each point of the triangle touches the circle. Color the triangle red. Fill in the rest of the space inside the circle with yellow. Print your name below the circle. Leave your paper on the upper left-hand side of your desk. _____ (insert a student's name) will collect the papers and bring them to me.

10. Get a piece of lined paper. Get out your crayon. Draw a rectangle on the paper. Inside the rectangle, draw a smaller rectangle. Write your name in red inside the small rectangle. Write today's date in blue above the large rectangle. Find the DIRECTIONS basket and put your paper in it.

11. On a piece of drawing paper, draw an imaginary animal. Write three sentences telling your animal's name, where it lives, and what it likes to eat. Write your name above your picture. Show your picture to a person near you. Write that person's name below your picture. Then put your paper in the DIRECTIONS basket.

12. On any kind of paper, draw a picture of yourself. To the right of your picture, write three words that describe you. Write your name at the bottom of your paper in the right-hand corner. Leave your paper on the upper right-hand side of your desk. _____ (insert a student's name) will collect the papers and bring them to me.

13. Look around the room at the different colors people are wearing. Count the number of boys wearing something blue and the number of girls wearing something blue. Write a sentence that tells how many boys you counted and how many girls. Write a second sentence to tell how many boys and girls in total are wearing something blue. Write your name at the top of your paper. Read your sentences to a person sitting near you. Then put your paper in the DIRECTIONS basket.

Follow the Directions! Joyful Learning

14. Find an example of something in the room that is shaped like a triangle. Draw a picture of it and write the name of the thing next to your drawing. Below your drawing write two sentences that describe it. Write your name to the left of your drawing. Put your paper in the DIRECTIONS basket.

15. Get out your crayons and a piece of paper. Draw a triangle on the paper. Inside the triangle draw a circle. Draw a circle around the triangle that does not touch the triangle anywhere. Color the inside of the small circle blue. Color the inside of the triangle red. Color the inside of the large circle green. Write your name at the top of the paper. Leave your paper on the upper left-hand side of your desk. _____ (insert a student's name) will collect the papers and bring them to me.

16. In the room, look for two things in the shape of a rectangle, two things in the shape of a circle, and two things in the shape of a triangle. Write three sentences to describe the things you observed. Write your name at the bottom of the paper. Put your paper in the DIRECTIONS basket.

TEACHER NOTE: Put a stack of note cards on your desk for this activity.
17. Get a note card from my desk. Write the word OLD at the top of the card. Underneath that word, write five words that rhyme with OLD. Put your name on the other side of the card and draw a triangle around it. When you have finished, pass your card to the person behind you (next to you). I will collect the cards.

TEACHER NOTE: On the chalkboard, print this message and enclose it in a box: "You are getting really good at following directions!"
18. Look at the words in the box on the board. Count how many words there are in the box. Write a sentence telling how many words are in the box. Write your name below your sentence. Read your sentence aloud to someone near you. I will collect your papers.

19. Draw a circle on a piece of notebook paper.
Draw a face inside the circle to show how you are feeling today. Below your face, write a sentence that tells how you are feeling. Write your name to the right of your drawing. Put your paper in the DIRECTIONS basket.

20. What is one kind of food that you like a lot? Write the name of the food at the top of your paper. Write three sentences telling about the food you like and why you like it. Turn to someone near you. Read your sentences to each other. Write both your names at the bottom of each paper, then put your paper in the DIRECTIONS basket.

> Peanut Butter
> I like peanut butter very much because it tastes so good with different foods. It's yummy on a banana with a glass of milk. My mom and dad put it with bacon and lettuce on white toast, and it makes a delicious sandwich.
>   Sam G.   Sally S.

Follow the Directions! Joyful Learning

MONTH 3

FOCUS Students follow more challenging directions that involve use of subject-area concepts. Additional challenges involve increased variations in the way the directions are posted and in where students put their completed papers. If your students are sitting at tables, be sure to assign them a number. They will be collecting each other's papers based on this number. If they are seated in rows, they will be collecting each other's papers based on their location.

TO DO

- Leave the DIRECTIONS sign or banner in the two current places and put a sign up in a third place.
- Tell students the directions will be posted each day in one of those three places.
- Write DIRECTIONS on the front of a manila folder in large, clear letters.
- Tell students that they will sometimes need to put their papers in the folder, sometimes in the basket, and sometimes do something else with them.
- When you use the folder or basket, put it in different places from time to time so that students must look around the room for it.

1. Choose two spelling words. Use each word in a sentence. Write your name underneath your sentences. Find the folder that says DIRECTIONS and put your paper there.

2. Choose one spelling word. Print the word down the left side of the page, putting one letter on each line. Next to each letter write a word that starts with that letter. Sign your name at the bottom. Find the DIRECTIONS basket and put your paper there.

3. Write five addition problems along with the answers. Each problem must have the numeral 7 somewhere in the problem or the answer. Each problem must be different from the others. Sign your name at the top. Put your paper on the upper right-hand corner of your desk. The first person in each row (one person from each table) should collect the papers from your row (table) and bring them to me.

4. Make up a word problem that uses the numerals 4 and 8. You can use other numerals, too, if you want to. Write your problem on a piece of notebook paper. Write the answer at the bottom of the page, and put your name at the top. Put your paper in the DIRECTIONS folder.

> Samantha Hogarth
> Jessica picked a dozen daisies. Four were white. Eight were yellow. How many more white daisies would she need to pick to have twice as many white daisies as yellow daisies?
> answer: 12

14

Follow the Directions! Joyful Learning

TEACHER NOTE: Use a map of your own choosing (with a legend) for this activity.

5. Study the map. Find two symbols on the map. Write the symbols on a piece of paper. Next to each one write a sentence telling what the symbol means. Put your name at the bottom of the paper, and put your paper in the DIRECTIONS basket.

6. Open your reading book to page 35. Look for words that rhyme with CAT. Write any words you find in a column on a piece of paper. Write your name at the top of the page in the middle, and place your paper in the DIRECTIONS basket.

7. Write these letters on your paper, one underneath the other: D G T L S. Next to each letter, write a noun that starts with that letter. Put your name underneath the last noun, and put your paper in the DIRECTIONS folder.

```
D. dragon
G. garden
T television
L lion
S shirt
Samuel
```

8. Make up a word problem that uses 9 and 4 and any other numbers you want. Write the answer on the back of the page, and write your name underneath the answer. Leave your paper on the upper right-hand corner of your desk. The last person in each row (person #4 from each table) should collect the papers from your row (table) and put the papers in the DIRECTIONS folder.

TEACHER NOTE: If you do not have enough dictionaries, photocopy and distribute the reproducibles on pages 78–79.

9. Open your dictionary to page 30. Find the first entry on page 30. Write a sentence using that word. Underline the word in the sentence. Write your name at the top of the page. Put your paper in the DIRECTIONS basket.

10. Count how many girls are wearing something blue today and how many boys are wearing something blue. Make a chart to show your findings. Put your name beneath the chart. Turn to the person next to you (behind you). Read your sentences to each other. Then place your paper in the DIRECTIONS folder.

11. Write these letters on your paper, one underneath the other: N B M C J. Next to each letter, write a verb that starts with that letter. Put your name underneath the last verb. Leave your paper on the upper right-hand corner of your desk. The third person in each row (one person from each table) should collect the papers from your row (table).

12. Make up a word problem that has to do with cookies. Your problem can have as many numerals as you want, but it must have the numerals 6 and 12. Write the answer beneath the problem, and write your name beneath the answer. Place your paper in the DIRECTIONS basket.

Follow the Directions! Joyful Learning

TEACHER NOTE: Students will need a map of their state for this activity.

13. On a map of your state, find two cities that are more than 35 miles from where you live. Write the names of the cities on your paper, and put your name at the top. Put your paper in the DIRECTIONS folder.

14. Write five math symbols on your paper, one underneath the other. Next to each symbol, write what the symbol means. (Example: + This means add.) Put your name at the top of the paper, and place your paper in the DIRECTIONS basket.

15. Draw a map of this classroom. Label your desk and four other things. Put your name above your map on the left side of the page, and put your paper in the DIRECTIONS folder.

16. Count how many girls are wearing something red today and how many boys are wearing something red. Make a chart to show your findings. Put your name beneath the chart. Turn to the person next to you and show him or her your chart. Then put your paper in the DIRECTIONS folder.

17. Make up three multiplication problems using only the numerals 2, 3, 4, and 5. (Example: 2 x 3 = ?) Each problem should have a different answer. Number the problems 1, 2, and 3. At the bottom of the page, make an answer key. Write your name at the top of the page, and put your paper on the upper left-hand side of your desk. _____ (insert student name) will collect the papers and put them in the DIRECTIONS folder.

18. Print the word DIRECTIONS on your paper. Write five words underneath DIRECTIONS using only the letters from the word DIRECTIONS; for example, you can make NET out of the letters E, T, and N. Write more words if you can think of more! Put your name at the top of your paper. Leave your paper on your desk. I will collect the papers.

19. Make up four multiplication problems using only the numerals 2, 4, 6, and 8. (Example: 2 x 4 = ?) Each problem should have a different answer. Number the problems 1 through 4. At the bottom of the page make an answer key. Write your name at the top of the page and put your paper in the DIRECTIONS folder.

20. Make up a word problem about pennies, nickels, and dimes. On the back of the page write the answer and explain how to solve the problem. Write your name on the front of the paper and put your paper in the DIRECTIONS basket.

MONTH 4

FOCUS Students continue following directions for relatively simple academic tasks, but the directions are now on individual worksheets. Students can do their work on these sheets, on the back of these sheets, or on separate sheets of paper, as they are expected to do on tests. Additional challenges involve students picking up their own DIRECTIONS activity each day from a central location and leaving the completed papers in one of two places or having them collected in different ways.

TO DO

- Set up a tray or box with a sign that says DIRECTIONS ACTIVITY FOR TODAY. TAKE ONE AND DO IT.

- Put the day's activity in the tray first thing in the morning, after recess, or at whatever time you prefer.

- Tell students the activities this month will include information on putting their completed papers in the DIRECTIONS folder or basket, as before, or having them collected in other ways.

REPRODUCIBLE

 **1.** Write the letter that comes next in this sequence, and explain what the pattern is. Then use the same letters to make up a different pattern. Write your name below your pattern and put the paper in the DIRECTIONS folder.

ABCAABCBABCCABC ___

Explanation: _____

My pattern _____

- -

 **2.** Draw a map below to show how to get from the main office to this classroom. Label the main office, this classroom, and any other important points along the way. Print your name on top at the left. Put your completed paper in the DIRECTIONS basket.

18

Follow the Directions! Joyful Learning

REPRODUCIBLE

 **3.** Print the letters of your first name below, one underneath the other. Next to each letter, write a verb that starts with that letter. You may use the dictionary to find verbs. Put your completed paper in the DIRECTIONS folder.

---

4. Read this sentence: HARLEY PYTHON WALKED INTO THE CLASSROOM. Now write it below, making two changes: (1) replace "Harley" with your own name, and (2) add a phrase to the end of the sentence to tell when you walked into the room. put the paper in the DIRECTIONS basket.

REPRODUCIBLE

 **5.** Open your reading book to page 49. Look for words that rhyme with CAN. In the space below write any words you find. Write your name at the top in the middle and place your paper in the DIRECTIONS folder.

- -

 **6.** Make up a word problem that involves a cake and that uses the numerals 4 and 5. You can use other objects and other numerals too, if you want to. Write your problem below and write the answer below the problem. Put your name at the top and place your paper in the DIRECTIONS basket.

REPRODUCIBLE

7. Write the next three letters in this sequence, and explain what the pattern is. Then use three or more letters to make up a different pattern. Put your name below your pattern. _____ and _____ will collect the papers and put them in the DIRECTIONS folder.

ABCBCDCDEDEF

Explanation: _____

My pattern: _____

- -

8. Count the number of boys in the class who are wearing blue, then the number wearing yellow, then the number wearing red. Do the same for the girls. Make a chart below to show what you found. Put your name below your chart. Leave your paper on your desk. _____ will collect them and put them in the same spot where they were left yesterday.

REPRODUCIBLE

9. Read these sentences: HARLEY PYTHON AND MARLEY GILL SPENT ALL AFTERNOON PLAYING KICKBALL. THEY WENT TO HARLEY'S HOUSE AND HAD A SNACK. Now write the sentences again making these changes: (1) Replace the names with your name and the name of your friend. (2) Replace "kickball" with your favorite sport. (3) Replace "a snack" with three of your favorite snacks. Put your paper in the DIRECTIONS basket.

10. List three of your favorite foods below, and list the same number of your favorite people. Then write three sentences, using the words in your lists. Each sentence must mention a different favorite food and favorite person. Write your name below the sentences.
Then put your paper in the DIRECTIONS basket.

11. Write the letters of your name on the back of this sheet, one underneath the other. After each letter, write a noun that starts with that letter. Use the letters of your name as the first letters of the words. Write your name at the top and put your paper in the DIRECTIONS folder.

22

Follow the Directions! Joyful Learning

REPRODUCIBLE

 **12.** Read this sentence: THE CAT JUMPED INTO THE BASKET. Now write the sentence below, making three changes: (1) Add a word to describe the cat. (2) Add a word after "jump" to tell how the cat jumped. (3) Add a word to describe the basket. Print your name at the top. Put your paper in the DIRECTIONS folder.

 **13.** Make up a word problem that involves going to the movies and that uses the numerals 2, 3, and 8, and others too, as you wish. Write your problem below, along with the answer. Put your name at the top and place your paper in the DIRECTIONS basket.

(on back)

 **14.** Write these words in a column in alphabetical order: green, beautiful, frog, mountain, raccoon, computer, books, sunshine. Put your name at the top of the column.

Put the paper in the DIRECTIONS basket.

Follow the Directions! Joyful Learning   23

REPRODUCIBLE

15. Below write at least five words of at least two letters using the letters in DIRECTIONS. For example, you can make NO from the letters O and N. You may use a letter twice in a word only if it appears twice in DIRECTIONS. Write more than five words if you can think of more! Put your name at the top of your paper, and give your paper to the person collecting the DIRECTIONS papers for today, who is _____ (insert student's name).

TEACHER NOTE: If you do not have enough dictionaries, photocopy and distribute the dictionary reproducibles on pages 78–79.

16. Open your dictionary to page 104 and find the last entry on that page. Below, write a sentence using that word. Underline that word in the sentence. Write your name at the top and put your paper in the DIRECTIONS basket.

TEACHER NOTE: If you do not have enough dictionaries, photocopy and distribute the dictionary reproducibles on pages 78–79.

17. Open your dictionary to page 82. Find the first and last entries on that page. Use each of the words in a sentence. Write your name at the top of the paper. Pass your paper to a person near you and have that person write his name at the bottom of your paper.

REPRODUCIBLE

18. Here are some letters: T F B D R A T R. Below write a sentence in which the words start with these letters in the order in which they appear here. For example, a sentence might start with the words "Tom's funny brother...." Write your name at the top of your paper and put it in the DIRECTIONS basket.

19. Make up a word problem about buying food. Include your name and the numerals 6, 7, and 8. You can use other numerals too, if you want to. Write your problem below, and include the answer. Put your paper in the DIRECTIONS folder.

---

20. Write the letter that comes next in the sequence below, and explain what the pattern is. Then use other letters to make up a different pattern. Write your name below your pattern. Pass your paper to a person near you and have that person write her name underneath yours. I will collect the papers.

A B A B B A B B B A B B B ___

Explanation: _____

My pattern: _____

Follow the Directions! Joyful Learning   25

MONTH 5

FOCUS Students follow more complicated, multi-step directions, many of which require interpreting information in charts, maps, and other graphic displays or creating such displays from text information. Students can do the activity on that same paper or on a separate sheet if they need more room.

TO DO

- Place the DIRECTIONS papers in a tray or box, as before, for students to pick up. Use the basket or folder for holding completed papers.

- Several activities in this section direct students to give their papers to a designated paper collector for the day. Near where you put out the activities for pick-up, post a sign indicating who the paper collector is for the day, if there is one. Rotate the job among students or others who may be in the classroom, such as aides or volunteers.

- Tell students that the designated person should always give the collected papers to you unless the directions say otherwise. Some activities include other ways of collecting the papers that may require a small amount of advance preparation.

REPRODUCIBLE

TEACHER NOTE: Use the map on page 73 or a U.S. map of your own choosing.

 **1.** Look at the maps of New York and California and locate two rivers in each state. Write at least two sentences below telling about the rivers that you found. Put your name at the top and give your paper to the person collecting the DIRECTIONS papers for today.

TEACHER NOTE: For this activity, have students work in pairs. Make copies of the weather map on page 77 or bring in copies of a weather map of your choosing.

  **2.** With a partner, study the weather map. Choose one city to study. What are the high and low temperatures forecast for that city? What else does the map tell about the weather in that city? Write what you learn below, put both your names on the paper, and give it to the person collecting the DIRECTIONS papers for today.

Follow the Directions! Joyful Learning

27

REPRODUCIBLE

3. Study this chart. Write one sentence that describes what the chart is about overall. Then write at least three more sentences about the different things the chart tells you. Put your name at the bottom of your paper. Put your paper in the DIRECTIONS basket.

Students	Nonfiction books read this month	Fiction books read this month
Amy	2	5
Phil	4	1
Sue	5	3
Willie	2	1

4. Pretend you are a newspaper sports reporter. Here are the scores you jotted down from three basketball games that were played one night. On a piece of notebook paper write a brief paragraph that tells which teams won, which game had the closest final score, and which team scored the most total points. Give your article a headline, and put your name below it. Be prepared to read your article to the class if I call your name. I will collect your papers.

Scouts   85
Sharks   79

Cardinals   63
Jays   52

Lions   88
Bears   86

REPRODUCIBLE

5. Some students observed what the class hamsters ate for a week and made graph to show what they saw. Here it is. Summarize what it tells in a paragraph. Put your paper in the DIRECTIONS basket. Reminder: Put your name on your paper!

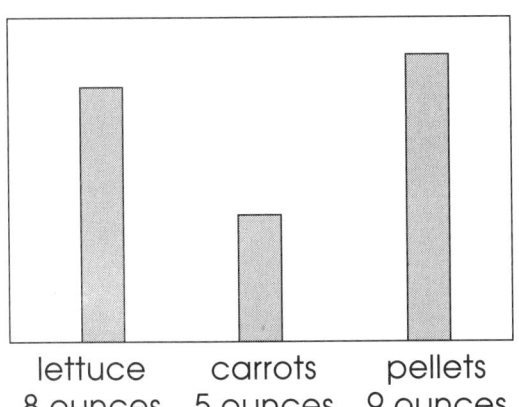

lettuce   carrots   pellets
8 ounces   5 ounces   9 ounces

- -

Teacher Note: Have students all use the same book for this activity. It can be any book if they do not all have the same reading book.

6. Open your reading book to page 75. Count the number of full paragraphs on the page. Do the same for pages 76, 77, and 78. Make a graph below to show your findings. Put your paper on the upper left-hand side of your desk. _____ will collect the papers and put them in the DIRECTIONS folder. Don't forget to put your name on your paper!

Follow the Directions! Joyful Learning

REPRODUCIBLE

TEACHER NOTE: Use the map on page 71 for this activity or a map of your own choosing.

7. On the map of North America, locate the country of Canada and find the names of three Canadian cities that are near large bodies of water. Write a paragraph below telling which cities you found and what body of water each one is near. Put your name at the end of your paragraph. I will collect the papers.

REPRODUCIBLE

8. Some students surveyed their classmates to find out which of six school lunches they liked best. They made a graph to show what they learned. Here it is. Write a few sentences on the back that tell at least four things this graph tells about the students.

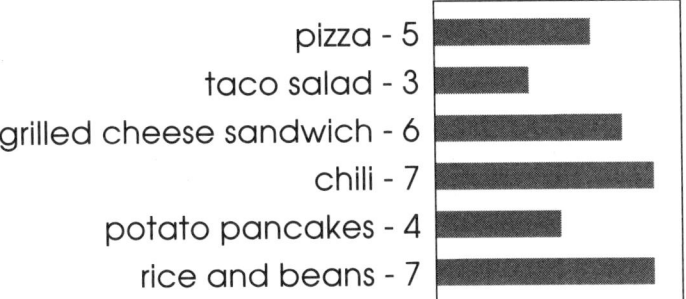

Don't forget to put your name on your paper!

9. Here is a chart that shows how four different school soccer teams stand in the middle of the season. Pretend you are a sports reporter and write a short article about the teams based on the information in the chart. Sign your name to your article. Be prepared to read your article to the class if I call your name. I will collect the papers.

TEAM	WINS	LOSSES
Runners	7	2
Champs	6	3
Blues	2	7
Rovers	3	6

Follow the Directions! Joyful Learning

REPRODUCIBLE

10. Make up a word problem about yourself saving money for something you want to buy. Your problem must include the total amount of the item, and it must use multiplication at some point. Write your problem below, and include the answer. Pass your paper to the front of your row (head of the table). _____ and _____ will collect the papers and put them in the DIRECTIONS folder.

---

11. Here are some letters: A T G R W A L. Below write a sentence in which the words start with these letters in the order in which they appear here. For example, a sentence might start "At the garage...." Write your name at the top and give your paper to the person collecting the DIRECTIONS papers for today.

REPRODUCIBLE

 **12.** Look around the room at the different colors people are wearing. Count the number of people wearing something red, the number wearing something blue, the number wearing something yellow, and the number wearing something green. Count each person only once. Make a bar graph to show your findings. Print your name at the top of the paper. When you are finished, bring your paper to me.

- -

TEACHER NOTE: Use the map on page 72 or supply your own map of a country other than the United States.

 **13.** On the map, find the names of three cities in that country and two other pieces of information about the country; for example, the names of rivers or mountain ranges. Write a paragraph telling the information you found. Put your name at the top and give your paper to the person collecting the DIRECTIONS papers for today.

REPRODUCIBLE

TEACHER NOTE: If you do not have enough dictionaries, photocopy and distribute the reproducibles on pages 78–79.

 **14.** Open your dictionary to any page on which you see one or more pictures. Write about a word that is pictured, explaining what it means. Be sure to tell what page you found the pictured word on. Write your name at the top. Put your paper in the DIRECTIONS basket.

 **15.** Look at the word SUPERMARKET. You can make lots of different words by using some of the letters in SUPERMARKET. Below write at least five words using only letters from the word SUPERMARKET. Each word must have at least three letters in it. For example, you can make ART from the letters A, R, and T. You may use a letter twice in a word only if it appears twice in SUPERMARKET. Write more than five words if you can think of more! Put your name at the top of your paper and put your paper in the DIRECTIONS basket.

TEACHER NOTE: Use the map on page 70 or supply your own map of the United States.

 **16.** On the map of the United States, locate the city of Chicago, and find the name of the lake that is closest to the city. Do the same for Detroit. Write a sentence below telling what you found out. Put your name at the top and place your paper in the DIRECTIONS folder.

REPRODUCIBLE

17. Look around the room at the colors of shirts or sweaters that people are wearing. Choose three colors. Count the number of people wearing tops of each color, and make a graph below to show your findings. On the back of your paper write one question that someone could answer by looking at your graph. Write your name below your question and give your paper to the person collecting the DIRECTIONS papers for today.

18. Make up a word problem about going on a trip. Include your name and the numerals 4, 7, and 50. You can use other numerals too, if you wish. Write your problem below, and include the answer. Put your name at the bottom, and give your paper to the person collecting the DIRECTIONS papers for today.

REPRODUCIBLE

TEACHER NOTE: Use the map on page 71 or supply your own map of the United States and Canada.

 **19.** On the map, find the border between the United States and Canada. Below write the names of two Canadian cities and two United States cities that are near the border. Put your name at the bottom of the paper and give it to the person collecting the DIRECTIONS papers for today.

 **20.** Some students surveyed their classmates to find out which of five school lunches they liked best. They made a graph to show what they learned. Here it is. On the back of your paper write a paragraph that tells at least four different things this graph tells about the students. Put your paper in the DIRECTIONS folder. Don't forget to put your name on your paper!

macaroni and cheese - 6 people
submarine sandwich - 8 people
corn pancakes - 2 people
hamburger and fries - 5 people
sloppy joe sandwiches - 8 people

36

Follow the Directions! Joyful Learning

MONTH 6

FOCUS Students continue following complicated, multi-step directions. Some of these require interpreting information in charts, maps, and other graphic displays, and some involve creating displays by interpreting text information. Students again pick up a paper on which the directions are written and do the activity on that same paper or a separate sheet if they need more room. A new procedure is that students start working with partners to complete some of the activities.

TO DO

- Place the directions papers in a tray or box, as before, for pickup by students.
- Use the directions folder or basket for collecting completed papers.
- Post a sign indicating who the paper collector is for the day, if there is one. Rotate the job among students or others who may be in the classroom, such as aides or volunteers.
- Decide how you want to set up partnerships for activities that are to be done with partners. You may want to assign permanent partners or use your own way of pairing students up each time.

REPRODUCIBLE

1. On the right side of this paper, in a column, list ten animals that you like. On the right side of your list, in a column, alphabetize the words on your list. In your alphabetized list, circle the animal that you like the best. On the back of your paper write four sentences about the animal you circled. Put your name at the top of the paper.

---

2. Draw a square below. Inside the square, write the numeral 20. On each side of the square, on the outside, write a different number sentence in which 20 is the answer. For example, 10 + 10 = 20. Put your name below the square.

REPRODUCIBLE

3. Here are some different kinds of foods. On a separate sheet of paper, put the foods in three columns: Meats, Vegetables, and Fruits. Write the name of the group at the top of each the column. Below the columns, write a paragraph telling what you would want to have in a meal, choosing only from these foods. Put your name at the top of the paper. When you are finished, bring your paper to me.

peas	green beans	apples	cherries
chicken	bananas	carrots	potatoes
oranges	ground beef	turkey	ham

---

4. Some students surveyed their classmates to find out what they usually do right after school. They made a graph to show what they learned. Here it is. Below the graph, write a paragraph that tells three things based on information in the graph. For example, the graph shows that four people do homework after school. Give your paper to the person collecting the papers for today. Don't forget to put your name on your paper!

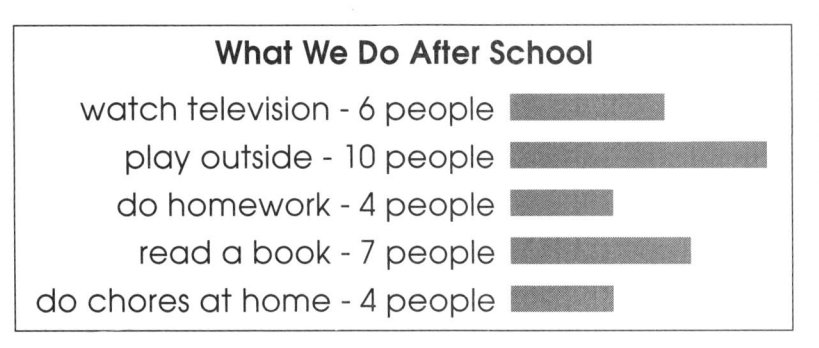

What We Do After School
watch television - 6 people
play outside - 10 people
do homework - 4 people
read a book - 7 people
do chores at home - 4 people

Follow the Directions! Joyful Learning

REPRODUCIBLE

TEACHER NOTE: Use the map on page 70 or a U.S. map of your own choosing.

5. On the United States map find all the states that are on Lake Michigan and list their names. Then, next to each of those names, write the name of the capital of that state. Write your name at the top of your paper and put it in the DIRECTIONS basket.

---

6. Draw four boxes below. Inside each one, write a number sentence that has an answer of 15. For example, 20 - 5 = 15. Each number sentence must be different from the other three, and only one may show addition. Outline each box in a different color. Put your name at the top of your paper. Leave your paper on the upper right-hand side of your desk. _____ will collect the papers and put them in the DIRECTIONS basket.

TEACHER NOTE: Use the map on page 70 or a U.S. map of your own choosing.

7. On a map of the United States find the Pacific Ocean. Make a list of all the states that have a coast on the Pacific Ocean. Then make a list of all the states that are next to the states on your first list. Put your name at the top of your paper and leave it on your desk. _____ will collect the papers and put them in the same spot as yesterday.

8. On a separate sheet of paper, draw four circles. Inside each one, write a number sentence that has an answer of 24. For example, 4 x 6 = 24. Each number sentence must be different from the other three, and each one must show a different arithmetic operation (add, subtract, multiply, divide). Put your name at the top of your paper.

TEACHER NOTE: Use the map of New York and California on page 73 and the U.S. map on page 70 or a U.S. map of your own choosing.

9. On the map choose one state to look at closely. Write the name of the state on a sheet of paper. Then write five things you learned about the state from reading the map. Put your name at the top of your paper.

---

10. A class in New York was talking about where they were born. One student kept notes on the board. Here's what the notes looked like at the end of the discussion. Make a bar graph to show how many students were born in each place. Put your name at the top.

Where We Were Born	
New York	9 students
New Jersey	5 students
California	2 students
Connecticut	6 students
Pennsylvania	4 students
Maryland	3 students

Follow the Directions! Joyful Learning

REPRODUCIBLE

TEACHER NOTE: Use the map on page 70 or bring in one or more road maps of your own choosing.

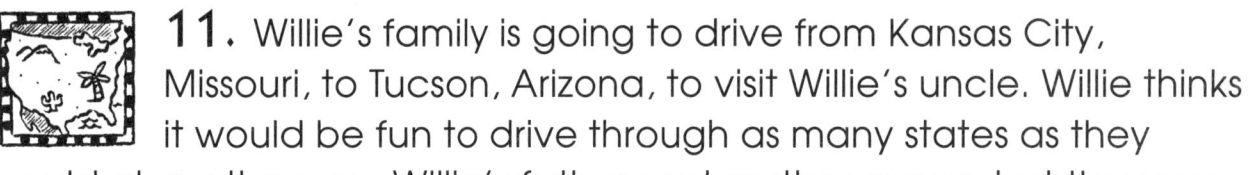

11. Willie's family is going to drive from Kansas City, Missouri, to Tucson, Arizona, to visit Willie's uncle. Willie thinks it would be fun to drive through as many states as they could along the way. Willie's father and mother agree, but they say, "We'll have to take a route that is as straight and direct as possible." Look at a map of the United States, and plan the best route for the family. List the states they will go through. Put your name at the top, and give your paper to the person collecting the papers for today.

---

12. Matt loved bananas, and his mother let him eat as many as he wanted. On Monday Matt ate five bananas. On Tuesday he ate six bananas. On Wednesday he ate three bananas. On Thursday he ate seven bananas. On Friday he ate five bananas. On Saturday he ate 10 bananas. On Sunday he ate 12 bananas. Then he said, "I love bananas, but I've had enough!" Make a chart to show Matt's banana-eating each day for the week. Then figure out how many bananas he ate altogether, and write that information in a sentence below your graph. Put your name at the top, and place your paper in the DIRECTIONS folder.

---

13. Sandy and Mandy loved to watch television, but their mother thought they watched it too much. The mother said, "From now on, you may watch only 10 hours of television each week, and you may watch no more than two hours of television a day. It's up to you to decide how you will use the ten hours." What would you do if you were Sandy and Mandy? Plan a week's schedule of television-watching for the girls that shows how much they may watch each day. Put your name at the top, and give it to the person collecting papers for today.

TEACHER NOTE: Use the weather map on page 77 or use a weather map of your own choosing.

14. With a partner, choose a location on the map and study the weather for that location. What are the high and low temperatures forecast? What else does the map tell about the weather? Write what you learned below, put your names on the paper, and put your paper in the DIRECTIONS basket.

- -

15. A class took a survey and made this chart to show the information they found. Write a paragraph that tells about four things you can learn from the chart; for example, five of the girls like best to play sports. Put your name at the top of your paper. Be ready to read your paragraph if I call your name.

OUR FAVORITE THINGS TO DO FOR FUN		
Favorite Acitivities	Boys	Girls
Play sports	4	5
Read	3	5
Watch television	4	4
Play video games	5	2

REPRODUCIBLE

TEACHER NOTE: Use the map on page 70 or use a map of your own choosing.

16. Willie's family is going to drive from Kansas City, Missouri, to Annapolis, Maryland, to visit Willie's grandmother. Willie thinks it would be fun to drive through as many states as possible along the way. Willie's mother and father agree, but they want to take a straight and direct route. Look at a map of the United States, and plan a route for the family. List the states the family would go through. Show your route to someone near you, and discuss how your routes are alike and different. Write both your names on each paper, then put your papers in the DIRECTIONS folder.

---

17. A class took a survey and made this chart to show what they found out. Working with a partner, write a paragraph that tells four comparisons you can make from studying the chart; for example, more boys like cereal for breakfast than toast and fruit. Put both your names at the top of your paper, and put it in the DIRECTIONS folder.

OUR FAVORITE BREAKFAST FOODS	Boys	Girls
Cereal and milk	4	3
Eggs and bacon	5	3
Toast and fruit	3	3
Pancakes	6	5

REPRODUCIBLE

18. Sally worked for six weeks walking people's dogs. She made $10 the first week, $12 the second week, $15 the third week, $9 the fourth week, $18 the fifth week, and $22 the sixth week. Make a graph to show Sally's earnings each week. Then figure out how much she made in total and write that information in a sentence below your graph. Put your name at the bottom of the paper and give it to the person collecting the DIRECTIONS papers for today.

---

19. Gregory loved apples, and his mother let him eat as many as he wanted. On Monday Gregory ate three apples. On Tuesday he ate five apples. On Wednesday he ate four apples. On Thursday he ate six apples. On Friday he ate five apples. On Saturday he ate nine apples. On Sunday he ate 10 apples. Then he said, "I love apples, but I've had enough!" Working with a partner, make a chart to show Gregory's apple-eating each day for the week. Then figure out how many apples he ate altogether, and write that information in a sentence below your graph. Put both your names on the paper, and put the paper in the DIRECTIONS basket.

TEACHER NOTE: Use the map on page 70 for this activity or use a road map of your own choosing.

20. Willie's family is going to drive from Kansas City, Missouri, to Seattle, Washington, to visit Willie's aunt. Willie thinks it would be fun to drive through as many states as they could along the way. Willie's mother and father agree, but they want to take a straight and direct route. Look at a map of the United States, and plan a route for the family that everyone will like. Describe your route in a paragraph, naming the states the family would go through. With a partner, compare your two routes, and write one sentence telling how your routes are alike. Put both your names on each of your papers, and put the papers in the DIRECTIONS folder.

Follow the Directions! Joyful Learning

MONTH 7

FOCUS Students follow more complicated, multi-step directions that require analysis of the information as well as basic interpretation. They will be working with a partner more often. They also have chances to represent more complicated information in a variety of ways.

TO DO

- Place the DIRECTIONS papers in a tray or box, as before, for pickup by students.
- Use the DIRECTIONS folder and basket for collecting completed papers, as before.
- Also as before, post a sign indicating who the paper-collector is for the day. Rotate the job among students or others who may be in the classroom, such as aides or volunteers.
- You may want to have students try writing some of the daily directions. Invite them to submit their ideas, and use a few if you think they'd be fun for the class to do.

REPRODUCIBLE

1. Some students surveyed their classmates to find out what kinds of books they like. They found out that five boys and four girls liked books about sports. Six boys and three girls liked science fiction books. Four boys and five girls liked true animal stories. Two boys and five girls liked realistic novels. With a partner make a bar graph on a separate sheet of paper to show this information. Make sure you show the details for girls and boys separately. Put your paper in the DIRECTIONS basket. Don't forget to put both your names on your paper!

TEACHER NOTE: Use the weather map on page 77 or use a national weather map.

2. Study the weather map to find out what the weather will be like in Chicago today. Write a paragraph that describes the weather and that also tells two things: (1) what kind of clothes people will be wearing in Chicago today and (2) what kind of things they might be doing outdoors; for example, if the temperature is very high, people would be wearing cool, cotton clothes and a lot of them might go swimming. Write your name at the top of your paper and put it in the DIRECTIONS basket.

---

3. You can make lots of different words by using the letters in BEAUTIFUL. For example, you can make FIT from the letters T, I, and F. Below write at least six words using letters from BEAUTIFUL. Each word must have at least two letters in it. You may use a letter twice in a word only if it appears twice in BEAUTIFUL. Write your name at the bottom of your paper. When you are finished, bring your paper to me.

Follow the Directions! Joyful Learning

TEACHER NOTE: Use the chart below or the master on page 80 for children's use in making their own pie charts.

4. Tim earns money every week by doing chores. Here's a pie chart showing what Tim did with his money last month. This month Tim saved half of his money and spent one fourth on the movies and one fourth on computer games. On a blank chart show what Tim did with his money this month. Label the sections of your chart. Write your name at the bottom of your paper and give it to the person collecting papers for today.

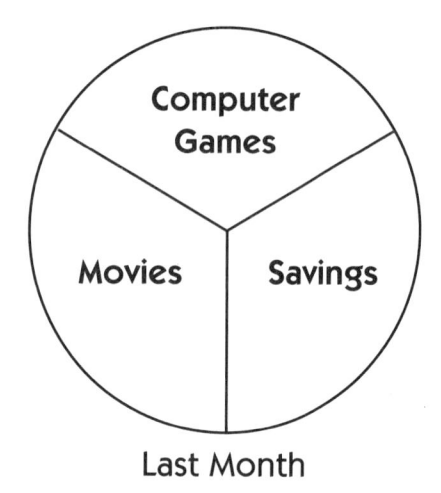

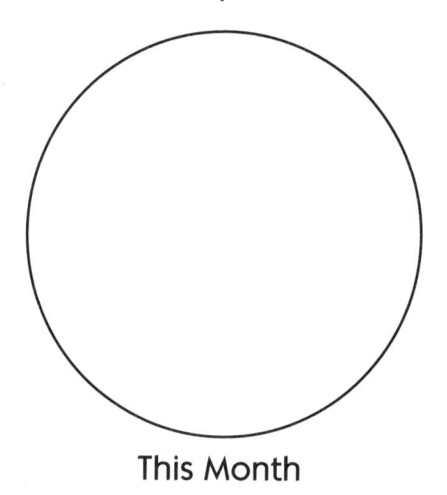

Last Month — Computer Games, Movies, Savings

This Month

---

5. One day Guffy's mother sent him to his grandmother's house with a big basket of apples. There were 20 apples in the basket when he left the house. Then he ran into Ralph and Jimmie and Chester, and they all wanted some apples, so he let each of them take a few. Ralph took three apples, Jimmie took two apples, and Chester took two apples. Then Ralph said he wanted to take two more for Larry, so Guffy gave him two more. Later on Guffy ran into Martha and Jennifer. They wanted some apples too, so Guffy let each of them take two. By that time, he was hungry, so he ate an apple himself. Then he went straight to his grandmother's house. Draw a picture that shows the basket and the number of apples in it when he gave it to his grandmother. Put your name at the top of the paper, and put it in the DIRECTIONS basket.

REPRODUCIBLE

6. A class took a survey of the kinds of foods everyone liked for breakfast. They found out that three boys liked cereal, six liked bacon and eggs, two liked toast, and five liked pancakes. Five girls liked cereal and milk, four liked bacon and eggs, four liked toast, and three liked pancakes. With a partner make a chart to show all this information. Then write a sentence that tells what the most popular and least popular foods are overall. Put your names at the top of your paper and give the paper to the person collecting DIRECTIONS papers.

---

7. On the left side of a separate sheet of paper, list ten animals that you think are interesting. On the right side, in a column, alphabetize the words on your list. In your alphabetized list, circle the two animals that you think are the most alike. Below the columns write a paragraph comparing the animals you circled. Tell at least three ways in which the animals are alike. Put your name at the top of the paper and place your paper in the DIRECTIONS basket.

TEACHER NOTE: Use the map of New York and California on page 73 and the U.S. map on page 70 or a U.S. map of your own choosing.

8. Using both sets of maps, compare the states of New York and California. In a paragraph explain three ways the states are alike. Put your name at the top and give your paper to the person collecting the DIRECTIONS papers for today.

Follow the Directions! Joyful Learning

9. One day Guffy decided to take some apples to his grandmother, and he left home with 25 apples in the basket. Before long he saw Martha and Jennifer, and they wanted some apples, so he let each one take two. Then Ralph and Jimmie and Chester came along, and they all wanted some apples. Ralph took as many as Martha had taken, and so did Jimmie. Chester wasn't very hungry, so he took only one apple. Guffy went on his way, but then he tripped and dropped the basket and five apples rolled down the hill. "Oh, well," thought Guffy, "I still have some left for Grandma." Draw a picture that shows the basket and the number of apples in it when he gave it to his grandmother. Put your name at the top of the paper and give it to the person collecting the papers for today.

---

10. Sukie worked for six weeks baby-sitting. She made $20 the first week, $20 the second week, $30 the third week, $10 the fourth week, $20 the fifth week, and $30 the sixth week. With a partner write a paragraph that tells about her earnings. First tell how much she made in total. Then make three comparisons between her earnings for different weeks; for example, you could say that Sukie made the same amount in the first week that she did in the second week. Put your names at the bottom of the paper. Put your paper in the DIRECTIONS basket.

---

11. Do this activity with a partner. On the left side of a piece of paper, in a column, list ten foods that you both like. On the right side, in another column, alphabetize the words on your list. In your alphabetized list, circle two foods that are alike. Write a paragraph telling at least three ways the foods are alike. Put your names at the top of the paper and give it to the person collecting the papers for today.

TEACHER NOTE: Use the map of New York and California on page 73 and the U.S. map on page 70 or a U.S. map of your own choosing.

12. With a partner, look at both sets of maps. In a paragraph, explain three ways the states are different. Put your names at the top and give your paper to the person collecting the DIRECTIONS papers for today.

---

13. Look at the word AIRPLANE. You can make lots of different words by using some of the letters in AIRPLANE. Below write at least five words using only letters from the word AIRPLANE. For example, you can make the word AIR from the letters A, I, and R. In your list, two words must have two letters in them, two words must have three letters, and one word must have four letters. Put your name at the top and give your paper to the person collecting the DIRECTIONS papers for today.

TEACHER NOTE: Use the map on page 70 or a U.S. map of your own choosing.

14. Look at a map of the United States. Choose two states to compare and contrast. In a paragraph explain two ways the states are alike and two ways they are different; for example, Iowa and Ohio are both north of Kentucky, but they are on opposite sides of the Mississippi River. Put your name at the top of your paper and leave it in the DIRECTIONS basket.

REPRODUCIBLE

TEACHER NOTE: Use the map on pages 74–75 or a world map of your own choosing.

15. With a partner look at a map of the world. Find the latitude line that is at 40 degrees north (above the equator). On that line, find one country in Europe and one country in Asia. Write "40 Degrees North Latitude" at the top of your paper. Then list the countries you found that are on that latitude line. Put your names at the top of the paper, and put your paper in the DIRECTIONS folder.

- -

16. Guffy set out for his grandmother's house with a basket of 15 apples. He stopped by the pasture to visit his horse and gave the animal two apples. Then along came Ralph and Jimmie and Chester, and they all wanted some apples. Ralph and Jimmie each took two. Chester was very hungry, so he took three apples. Guffy went on his way, and when he passed by an apple tree, he picked six apples and put them in the basket. Then Martha and Jennifer came along and just had to have some apples. He gave each girl one apple and then he went on to his grandmother's house and gave her all the rest. Write a sentence telling how many apples Guffy had for his grandmother when he got to her house. Put your name at the top of the paper, and put it in the DIRECTIONS folder.

- -

TEACHER NOTE: Use the map on pages 74–75 or a world map of your own choosing.

17. On the map of the world find the equator. Now find three countries that are on the equator. Each country must be in a different continent. For instance, you can't list two countries that are both in South America. Put your name at the top of the paper, and put your paper in the DIRECTIONS folder.

52

Follow the Directions! Joyful Learning

REPRODUCIBLE

TEACHER NOTE: Use the map on pages 74–75 or a world map of your own choosing.

18. With a partner, look at a map of the world. Find the latitude line that is at 20 degrees south (below the equator). Now find one country in South America that is on that line and one country in Africa that is on that line. Write "20 Degrees South Latitude" at the top of your paper. Then list the two countries you found that are on that latitude line. Put your names at the top of the paper and give it to the person collecting the papers for today.

---

19. Look at the word ELEPHANT. You can make lots of different words by using some of the letters in ELEPHANT; for example, you can make the word TAN from the letters A, N, and T. Below write at least six words of three letters each using letters from the word ELEPHANT. You may use a letter in a word as many times as it is used in ELEPHANT. Put your name at the bottom of the paper and give it to the person collecting papers for today.

---

20. Here are some different kinds of sports. Working with a partner, put the sports into two columns: sports you play with a ball and sports you play without a ball. Write the name of the group at the top of each column. Below the columns write a four-sentence paragraph telling which sport you like best and why. Put your names at the top of the paper and give it to the person collecting the papers for today.

baseball   wrestling
swimming   cycling
tennis   skiing
football   ice skating
basketball   soccer

Follow the Directions! Joyful Learning

MONTH 8

FOCUS Students continue with complicated, multi-step directions that include both text and graphic information (especially maps) and that require analysis of the information, as well as simple interpretation. Also, there are some activities that involve creating patterns and folding paper that will provide new and different challenges. For some activities students will work with a partner or a small group.

TO DO

- Place the DIRECTIONS papers in a tray or box, as before, for pickup by students.

- Use the DIRECTIONS folder and basket for collecting completed papers, as before.

- Also as before, post a sign indicating who the paper-collector is for the day. Rotate the job among students or others who may be in the classroom, such as aides or volunteers.

- You may want to have students continue suggesting some of the daily directions. Have them submit their ideas to you in writing; use the ones that are most clear and inventive.

REPRODUCIBLE

1. Think of two different letters—any letters except A and B. Now make up a pattern with those letters. For example, AABBAABB....Your pattern must use each letter at least four times in all and may not be the same as the example. Write your pattern on a separate sheet of paper. Then describe your pattern in a short paragraph. Put your name at the top of the paper and put your paper in the DIRECTIONS basket.

TEACHER NOTE: Use the master on page 80 for students' use in making their own pie charts.

2. Form a group of three to complete this activity. Mandy earns money every week by doing yard work in her neighborhood. Here's a pie chart showing what Mandy did with her money last month. This month Mandy spent half of her money on books and one fourth on movies. She saved the rest. Draw a chart that shows what Mandy did with her money this month, and label the sections of your chart. Write your names at the bottom of your paper. When you are finished, put your paper in the DIRECTIONS folder.

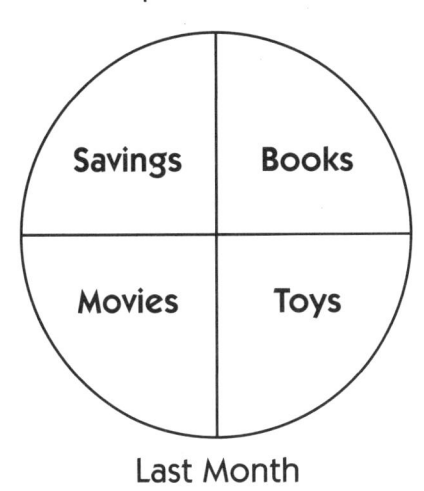

Savings	Books
Movies	Toys

Last Month

---

3. Fold a piece of notebook paper in half lengthwise. Place the paper on your desk so that the fold is on your left. Now fold the paper in half again by bringing the top edges over to meet the bottom edges. On the front of the folded paper you now have, print your first name. Now lift the top half up, and on the bottom half print your last name. Now open the paper completely. In the lower left-hand corner, write how old you are.
Fold the paper again. Put your paper in the DIRECTIONS basket.

REPRODUCIBLE

4. Work with a partner to complete this activity. You can make lots of different words by using the letters in TELEVISION. For example, you can make NET from the letters T, E, and N. Write six words of three letters each using letters from the word TELEVISION. Also write two words that have four letters each. In each word you may use a letter only as many times as it is used in TELEVISION; for instance, you may use the letter "e" only two times in a word because it is used two times in TELEVISION. Put your name at the top of your paper, and put your paper on the upper left-hand side of your desk. _____ will collect the papers and put them in the DIRECTIONS folder.

---

5. Once again Guffy set out for his grandmother's house with a basket of apples. He had 17 apples in the basket. A mile from his house he dropped the basket, and six apples rolled away. A half mile farther on he dropped the basket again, and three apples rolled away. A block from his grandmother's house he met Mrs. Core, who was coming back from the store with a large bag of apples, and he told her about dropping his basket. She felt sorry for him and put an apple in his basket. Guffy then went straight to his grandmother's house. Draw a picture that shows the basket and the number of apples in it when Guffy arrived at his grandmother's house. Put your name at the top of the paper. Leave your paper on your desk. _____ will collect them and put them on my desk.

REPRODUCIBLE

TEACHER NOTE: Use the map on page 70 or a U.S. map of your own choosing.

6. On a map of the United States find the state of Colorado and the states that border Colorado. Write the border states in a list under the heading "Neighbors of Colorado." Then find Denver, Colorado. If you go 600 miles directly south of Denver, what state will you be in? If you go 600 miles directly north of Denver, what state will you be in? Write the names of those two states under the heading "600 Miles From Denver." Put your name at the top of the paper and put your paper in the DIRECTIONS folder.

---

7. Fold a piece of notebook paper in half by bringing the top edge down to meet the bottom edge. Put the paper on your desk with the fold across the top. Now fold the paper in half again by bringing the left edges over to meet the right edges. On the front, print your first name and your last name. Now lift the left edge away from the right edge, and on the inside, on the left, write three words that start with the first letter of your first name. On the right, write three words that start with the first letter of your last name. Fold the paper back up so that your name is on the outside, and give it to the person who is collecting papers for today.

TEACHER NOTE: Use the map on page 70 or a map of your own choosing.

8. On a map of the United States, find Amarillo, Texas. Then find Sioux Falls, South Dakota. Where is Sioux Falls in relation to Amarillo? (That is, is it north? southeast? or some other direction?) How far is it between Amarillo and Sioux Falls as the crow flies? That means going in a straight line between the two cities. Tell how far it is in a sentence. What states does that straight line go through? Make a list of those states in order from south to north. Put your name at the top of the paper and put it in the DIRECTIONS folder.

Follow the Directions! Joyful Learning

REPRODUCIBLE

TEACHER NOTE: Use the map on pages 74–75 or a world map of your own choosing.

9. Look at a map of the world. Find the latitude line that is at 20 degrees north (above the equator). Now find one country in Africa and one country in Asia on the same line. Write "20 Degrees North Latitude" at the top of your paper. Then list the countries you found that are on that latitude line. Put your name at the top of the paper and put your paper in the DIRECTIONS basket.

TEACHER NOTE: Use the weather map on page 77 or a map of your own choosing.

10. With two other people study the weather map to see what today's weather will be like in San Francisco, California, and in Miami, Florida. Now draw two thermometers. On one show the expected high temperature for San Francisco for today. On the other, show the expected high temperature for Miami for today. Then, in two sentences, compare the weather in San Francisco and Miami to the weather in your town. Write your names at the top of your paper, and put your paper in the DIRECTIONS basket.

---

11. Put a piece of notebook paper on your desk with the lines going horizontal. Fold the paper in thirds by first bringing the bottom edge up and then bringing the top edge down over the bottom part that you just folded up. Place the paper on your desk with the top fold across the top. On the top flap print your first name and your last name. Now lift the top edge up, and on the folded-up bottom flap write the name of an animal that starts with the first letter of your first name. Now unfold the bottom flap. On the inside, on the middle third of the paper, write the name of an animal that starts with the first letter of your last name. Fold the paper again so that your name is on the outside and put your paper in the DIRECTIONS folder.

REPRODUCIBLE

12. Think of two different letters—any letters except A and B. Now make up a pattern with those letters. For example, ABBABBABBA.... Your pattern must use each letter at least six times in all and may not be the same as the example. Write your pattern and describe it in a short paragraph. Put your name at the top of the paper. Leave your paper on your desk. The person collecting papers today will pick the papers up and put them in the DIRECTIONS folder.

- -

13. Get two crayons or pencils of different colors. Make up a pattern with those colors by making a line of small, colored-in circles with the two different markers; for instance, one pattern might be RED, BLUE, RED, BLUE, RED, BLUE. (Your pattern must be different from this example.) Then describe your pattern in a short paragraph. Put your name at the top of the paper and leave it on your desk. The person collecting papers today will pick the papers up and put them in the DIRECTIONS folder.

- -

TEACHER NOTE: Use the master on page 80 for students' use in making their own pie charts.

14. Ralph earns money every week by helping his uncle on the farm. Here's a pie chart showing what Ralph did with his money last month. This month Ralph spent one fourth of his money on a radio and one fourth on a board game. He put the rest into his savings account. Draw a chart that shows what Ralph did with his money this month and label the sections of your chart. Write your name at the bottom of your paper and put your paper in the DIRECTIONS basket.

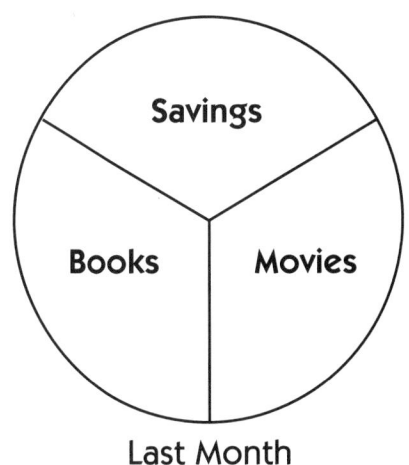

Savings / Books / Movies

Last Month

Follow the Directions! Joyful Learning

59

15. Fold a piece of notebook paper in half by bringing the top edge down to meet the bottom edge. Put the paper on your desk with the fold on the left. Now fold the paper in half again by bringing the top edge down to meet the bottom edge. On the front, draw a flower with a stem, leaves, and petals. Now lift the top edge, and on the inside write your first and last names. Underneath your name write the name of a flower that starts with the first letter of your first name or your last name. Now fold the paper again so that the flower is on the outside. Put your name at the top of the paper and leave it on your desk. The person collecting papers today will pick up the papers and put them in the DIRECTIONS basket.

TEACHER NOTE: Use the map on page 70 or a U.S. map of your own choosing.

16. Look at a map of the United States. Find the state of Missouri and the states that border it. Write the bordering states in a list under the heading "Neighbors of Missouri." Then find St. Louis, Missouri. If you go 600 miles directly west of St. Louis, what state will you be in? If you go 600 miles directly east of St. Louis, what state will you be in? Write the names of those two states under the heading "600 Miles From St. Louis." Put your name at the top of the paper and leave it on your desk. The person collecting papers today will pick up the papers and put them in the DIRECTIONS basket.

TEACHER NOTE: Use the map on page 70 or a U.S. map of your own choosing.

17. Look at a map of the United States. Find the state of Idaho and the states that border it. Write the bordering states in a list under the heading "Neighbors of Idaho." Then find Boise, Idaho. If you go 500 miles directly west of Boise, where will you be? If you go 500 miles directly east of Boise, where will you be? Explain in two sentences where you will be each time. Put your name at the top of the paper and put your paper in the DIRECTIONS basket.

REPRODUCIBLE

TEACHER NOTE: Use the weather maps on pages 76–77 or one of your own choosing.

18. Study the map to see what today's weather will be like in Chicago, Illinois, and in New York City, New York. Now draw two thermometers. On one show the expected high temperature for Chicago for today. On the other, show the expected high temperature for New York City for today. Then, in two sentences, compare the weather in Chicago and New York City to the weather where you live. Write your name at the top of your paper. Put your paper on the upper left-hand side of your desk. _____ will collect the papers and put them in the DIRECTIONS folder.

TEACHER NOTE: Use the weather map on page 77 or one of your own choosing.

19. Study the map to see what today's weather will be like in Atlanta, Georgia, and in Dodge City, Kansas. First, explain in writing how the weather in Atlanta compares to or contrasts with the weather in Dodge City. Then compare the weather in Atlanta and Dodge City for today to the weather where you live. Write your name at the top of your paper. Leave your paper on your desk. _____ will collect the papers and put them in the DIRECTIONS folder.

TEACHER NOTE: You'll need a large stack of magazines and newspapers for this activity. Use old ones that can be cut up.

20. With a partner, go through magazines or newspapers and find three pictures that relate to one another in some way. Paste the pictures on a sheet of paper. Underneath the pictures explain how they are related. Put your names at the top of the paper and give it to the person collecting papers for today.

Follow the Directions! Joyful Learning

MONTH 9

FOCUS Students continue with complicated, multi-step directions. Also, encourage students to continue proposing some of the daily directions. Have them submit their ideas in writing; use the ones that are most clear and inventive.

TO DO

- Place the DIRECTIONS papers in a tray or box, as before, for pickup by students.
- Use the DIRECTIONS folder and basket for collecting completed papers, as before.
- Also as before, post a sign indicating who the paper-collector is for the day. Rotate the job among students or others who may be in the classroom, such as aides or volunteers. For some activities, students will work with a partner or form small groups.

REPRODUCIBLE

1. Fold a piece of notebook paper in fourths by bringing the top edge down to meet the bottom edge and then bringing the fold at the top down to meet the bottom edge. Now unfold the paper so that the fold lines are horizontal on your desk. On the top fourth of the paper, write your first and last names. On the second fourth of the paper, write a sentence that tells about something you enjoy doing. On the third fourth, write your age and draw a row of five-pointed stars with the number of stars equaling your age. On the bottom fourth, write a number sentence that includes the number that stands for your age. Now fold the paper and give it to the person who is collecting papers for today.

TEACHER NOTE: Use the map on page 70 or a U.S. map of your own choosing.

2. On a map of the United States find the city of Charleston, West Virginia. If you go 300 miles due west of Charleston, where will you be? Make a note of that finding. Then figure out in what three places you will be if you go 300 miles due east, 300 miles south, and 300 miles north of Charleston. Explain all of your findings in four sentences. Then tell which of those four places you would most like to visit and why. Put your name at the top of the paper and put your paper in the DIRECTIONS basket.

---

3. A class of students sat in a circle and looked at their shoes. They found that 16 students were wearing sneakers, nine were wearing sandals, three were wearing hiking boots, and two were wearing moccasins. With a partner make a bar graph to show how many people were wearing each kind of shoe. Next, write three sentences describing the kinds of shoes that kids were wearing in the class. Then make three comparisons between the different kinds of shoes the students were wearing; for instance, you might compare the kind of shoe that most people wear with the kind that the fewest people wear. Put your names at the top of the paper. Be ready to read your answers if your name is called.

Follow the Directions! Joyful Learning

REPRODUCIBLE

4. Get or make a piece of paper that is in the shape of a square. Fold the top right corner down and over so that it touches the bottom left corner. Put the folded paper on your desk with the point facing you. Fold the point on the left over to meet the point on the right. On the top, write your name. Now open the paper so that you have only the first fold you made. On the inside list all the things you can think of that have a triangle in their shape. Fold the paper back up so that your name is on top. Leave your paper on the upper right-hand side of your desk. _____ will collect the papers and bring them to me.

TEACHER NOTE: Use the map on page 70 or a U.S. map of your own choosing.

5. Find the state of Wisconsin on the United States map. Notice what lake is on its eastern border. This is one of the Great Lakes. There are four other lakes in this group of lakes. Write the names of all five of them. Next to each one, write the name of a state that is bordered by that lake. Then choose two of the lakes and write two sentences that compare those lakes with each other. Put your name at the top of the paper. Share your answers with a partner, and have that person write her name on your paper below yours. When you are finished, put your paper in the DIRECTIONS folder.

TEACHER NOTE: Use the map on page 70 or a U.S. map of your own choosing.

6. On the map of the United States, find Salt Lake City, Utah. Then find Reno, Nevada. Where is Salt Lake City in relation to Reno? Explain this in a sentence. How far is it between Salt Lake City and Reno as the crow flies? Tell how far it is in a sentence. If you go 100 miles north of Salt Lake City, what state will you be in? If you go 100 miles south of Reno, what state will you be in? Explain your answers in sentences. Put your name at the top of the paper. Share your answers with a partner, and have that person write his or her name on your paper below yours. When you are finished, put your paper in the DIRECTIONS folder.

REPRODUCIBLE

7. Cut a circle from a piece of paper. In the center of the circle, write your name and draw a circle around it. Around your name list all the things you can think of that have the shape of a circle. You must list at least six things. Fold the circle in half and then in half again. Write your name on the outside. Give your paper to the person collecting papers for today.

TEACHER NOTE: Post a short article from a newspaper or magazine that students can read and that will work for this activity. Write above it the statement "Read this for your DIRECTIONS activity."

8. Look for the article you need for this activity. It's somewhere in the room. When you find it, read it. Then write three things the article tells. Write these things in your OWN words. Do not copy from the article. Next, write what you think of the information. Is it interesting? unusual? funny? or something else. Give reasons to support your answer. Put your name at the top of the paper, and put the paper in the DIRECTIONS basket.

---

9. Cut a triangle from a piece of paper. In each angle of the triangle, write one thing that has the shape of a triangle. In the middle of the triangle, write at least three other things that are shaped like a triangle. Turn the triangle over and write your name on that side. Put your completed triangle in the DIRECTIONS basket.

Follow the Directions! Joyful Learning

REPRODUCIBLE

TEACHER NOTE: Use the map on pages 74–75 or a world map of your own choosing.

10. With two other people, look at a map of the world. Find the latitude line that is at 30 degrees north (above the equator). Now find six countries that are on the same line. Write "30 Degrees North Latitude" at the top of your paper. Then list the countries you found that are on that latitude line. Put your names at the top of the paper. When you are finished, put your paper in the DIRECTIONS folder.

TEACHER NOTE: Use the map on page 70 or a U.S. map of your own choosing.

11. On a map of the United States find the city of Indianapolis, Indiana. How far is the Mississippi River from Indianapolis? Explain in a sentence. If you go 400 miles due west of Indianapolis, where will you be? Now figure out where you will be if you go 100 miles due east, 200 miles due south, and 300 miles due north of Indianapolis. Explain your findings in sentences. Then tell which of those four places you would most like to be and why. Put your name at the top of the paper. Put your paper in the DIRECTIONS basket.

TEACHER NOTE: Use the map on page 76 or a weather map of your own choosing.

12. Study the map to see what the weather will be like in Bridgeport, Connecticut. First, write a sentence that tells what the weather will be. Next, explain in writing how the weather in Bridgeport will be different from the weather in Atlantic City, New Jersey. Write your name at the top of your paper and put your paper on the upper left-hand side of your desk. _____ will collect the papers and put them in the DIRECTIONS folder.

13. Work with two other people to complete this activity. When Terry and her family visit San Francisco, they decide to take a ferry boat to Sausalito. They get to the dock at five minutes after noon and see this ferry schedule. What boat or boats could they take if they want to arrive back in San Francisco before 5:00 pm? How long will they be able to stay in Sausalito if their boat arrives 30 minutes after it leaves San Francisco? Write your answers in sentences. Then put your names at the top of your paper. When you are finished, put your paper in the DIRECTIONS folder.

| FERRY BOATS TO SAUSALITO ||
Leave At:	Return At:
9:00 am	10:00 am
10:30 am	11:30 am
noon	1:00 pm
1:30 pm	2:30 pm
4:30 pm	5:30 pm

TEACHER NOTE: You'll need a large stack of magazines and newspapers. Use old ones that can be cut up.

14. Work with a partner to do this activity. Go through some of the magazines or newspapers and find three pictures that relate to one another in some way. Paste the pictures on a sheet of paper. Underneath the pictures, explain how the pictures are related. Put your names at the bottom of the paper, and give it to the person collecting papers for today.

---

15. Fold a piece of notebook paper in thirds by bringing the top edge down and the bottom edge up. Now unfold the paper so that the fold lines are horizontal on your desk. On the top third of the paper, write your first and last names. On the middle third of the paper, write a sentence that tells about something you like to do. On the bottom third of the paper, write a word problem that uses the number "3." Now fold the paper back up, and give it to the person who is collecting papers for today.

REPRODUCIBLE

TEACHER NOTE: Use the map on page 76 or a weather map of your own choosing.

16. Study the weather map to see what the weather will be like in Morristown, New Jersey, tomorrow. First write a sentence that tells what the weather will be. Next, explain in writing how the weather in Montauk, New York, will be different from the weather in Morristown. Write your name at the top of your paper, and put your paper in the DIRECTIONS basket.

---

17. Mack and his family decide to take a bus from Weaverville to Mack's grandfather's house in Ford City. They study this bus schedule to plan their trip. What bus or buses could the family take if they want to arrive back home by 5:00 pm? How long will they be able to stay at Grandfather's house? Write your answers in sentences. Then put your name at the top of your paper and give it to the person collecting papers for today.

Leave Weaverville:	Arrive Ford City:
8:00 am	10:00 am
11:00 am	1:00 pm
2:00 pm	4:00 pm
5:00 pm	7:00 pm
Leave Ford City:	**Arrive Weaverville:**
7:00 am	9:00 am
10:00 am	noon
noon	3:00 pm
2:00 pm	5:00 pm
4:00 pm	6:00 pm

REPRODUCIBLE

18. Work with a partner on this activity. Susan and Betty are planning a party. They have decided to invite ten people, and they have $20.00 to spend. They go to a big store to get food and supplies. At the store, cookies cost $3.00 a dozen, ice cream costs $2.00 a gallon, and candy costs $3.00 for a bag of 30 pieces. Party favors are $1.00 a piece. How do you think they should spend their money? List the items you think they should buy, along with the cost of each and the total cost. Then explain how much of each thing each person would get at the party; for example, if you think the girls should buy a certain amount of candy, how much candy would each person be able to have? Write your names at the top of your paper and put it in the DIRECTIONS folder.

TEACHER NOTE: You'll need a large stack of magazines and newspapers. Use old ones that can be cut up.

19. Work with a partner on this activity. Go through some of the magazines or newspapers and find five pictures that relate to one another in some way. Paste the pictures on a sheet of paper. Underneath the pictures, explain how the pictures are related. Put your names at the top of the paper, and give it to the person collecting papers for today.

TEACHER NOTE: Use the map on page 70 or use a U.S. map of your own choosing.

20. On the map of the United States, find your home state. Plan a trip that will take you from your state to three different states and back home again. Below tell why you want to go to those three places and what you want to do when you get to each place. Then explain where you will go first, second, and third, and how far you will travel each time. Put your name at the top of the paper and put your paper in the DIRECTIONS folder.

Follow the Directions! Joyful Learning

REPRODUCIBLE

United States of America Map

70

Follow the Directions! Joyful Learning

REPRODUCIBLE

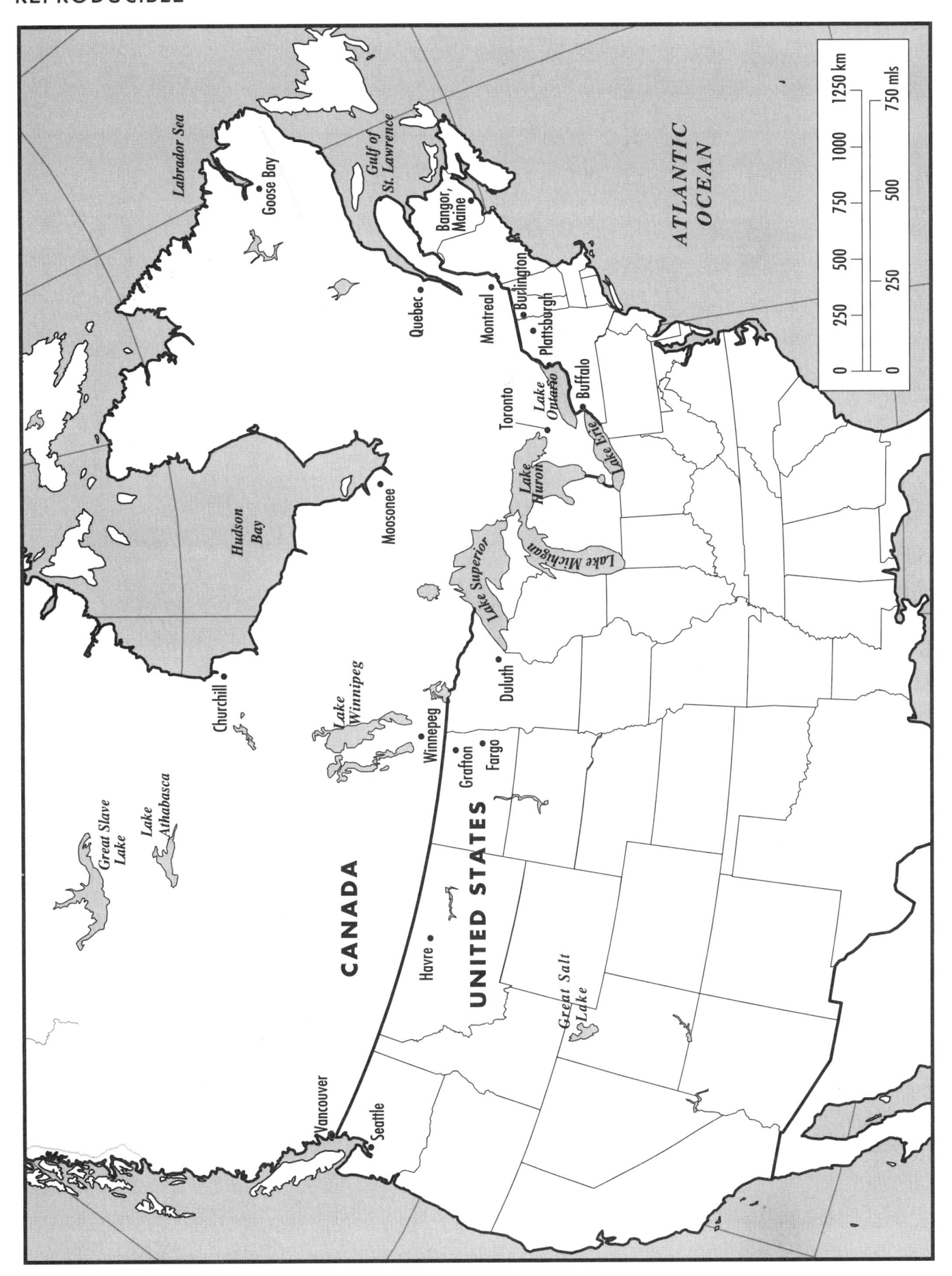

Labrador Sea
Goose Bay
Gulf of St. Lawrence
Bangor, Maine
Quebec
Montreal
Burlington
Plattsburgh
Buffalo
Toronto
Lake Ontario
Lake Erie
Lake Huron
Lake Superior
Lake Michigan

ATLANTIC OCEAN

Moosonee
Hudson Bay

Churchill
Lake Winnipeg
Winnipeg
Duluth
Grafton
Fargo

Great Slave Lake
Lake Athabasca

CANADA

Havre

UNITED STATES

Great Salt Lake

Vancouver
Seattle

| 0 | 250 | 500 | 750 | 1000 | 1250 km |
| 0 | 250 | 500 | 750 mls |

Follow the Directions! Joyful Learning

71

France

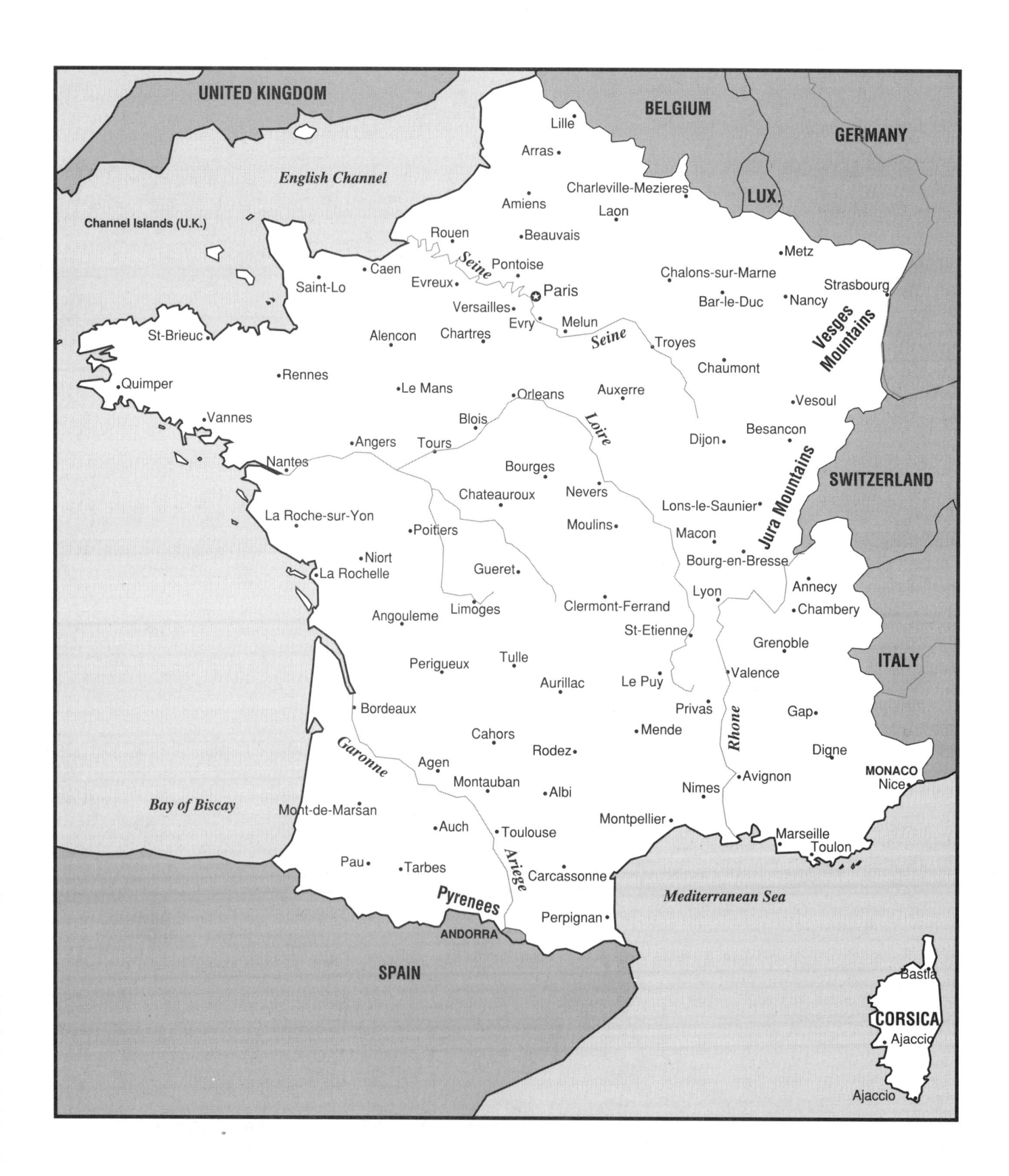

REPRODUCIBLE

New York

- Adirondack Mountains
- Albany
- *Hudson River*
- *Allegheny River*
- *Susquehanna River*
- New York City

California

- Klamath Mountains
- *Sacramento River*
- Sacramento
- San Francisco
- *San Joaquin River*
- *Salinas River*
- Death Valley
- Mohave Desert
- Los Angeles
- *Colorado River*
- San Diego

Follow the Directions! Joyful Learning

REPRODUCIBLE

World Map

1. Gabon
2. Congo
3. Singapore
4. Morocco
5. Jordan
6. Afghanistan
7. Pakistan
8. Nepal
9. Portugal
10. Italy
11. Armenia
12. Greece

74

Follow the Directions! Joyful Learning

REPRODUCIBLE

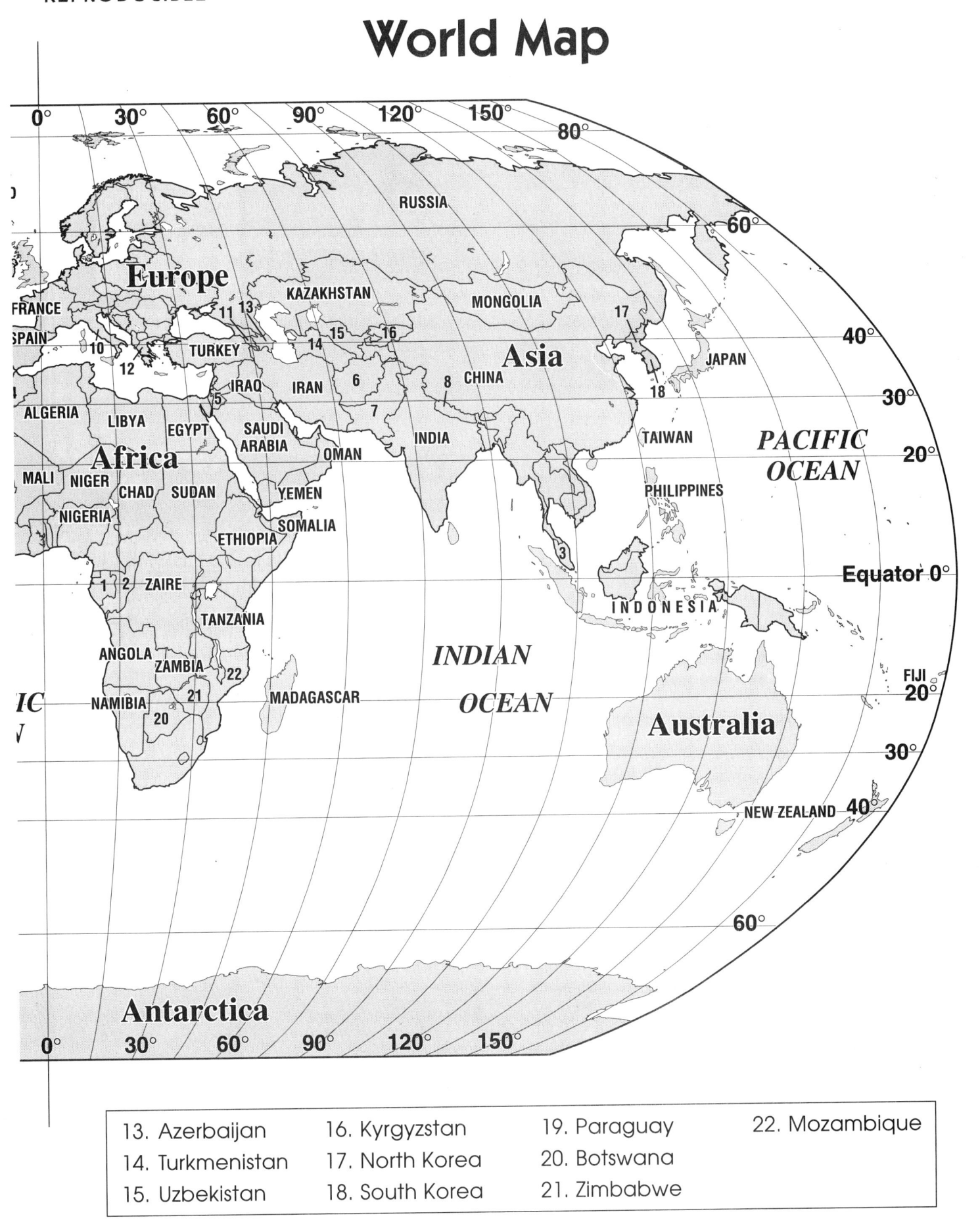

World Map

13. Azerbaijan	16. Kyrgyzstan	19. Paraguay	22. Mozambique
14. Turkmenistan	17. North Korea	20. Botswana	
15. Uzbekistan	18. South Korea	21. Zimbabwe	

Follow the Directions! Joyful Learning

REPRODUCIBLE

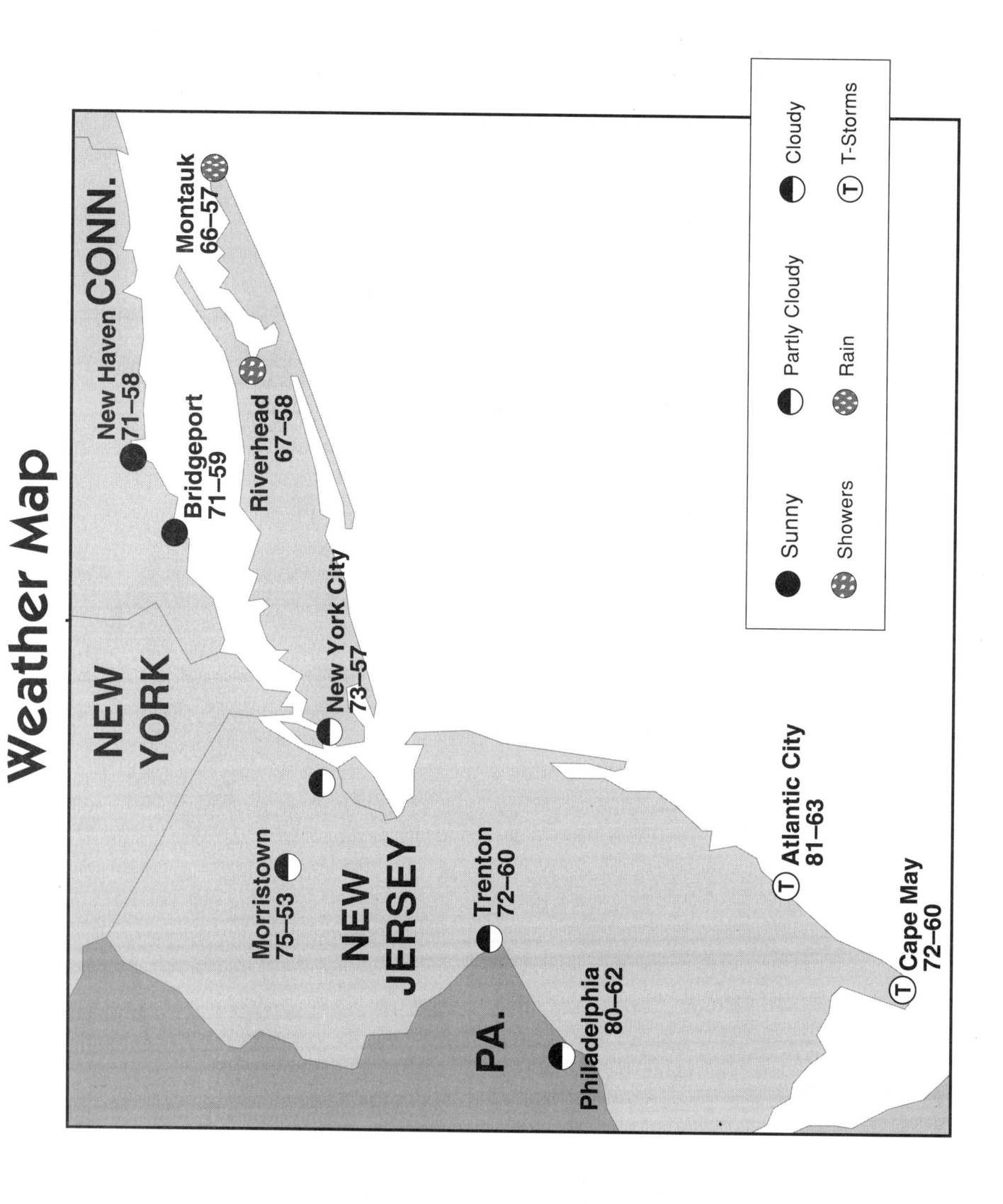

Weather Map

CONN.
New Haven 71–58
Bridgeport 71–59
Montauk 66–57
Riverhead 67–58

NEW YORK
New York City 73–57

NEW JERSEY
Morristown 75–53
Trenton 72–60
Atlantic City 81–63
Cape May 72–60

PA.
Philadelphia 80–62

Legend:
- Sunny
- Partly Cloudy
- Cloudy
- Showers
- Rain
- T-Storms

Follow the Directions! Joyful Learning

REPRODUCIBLE

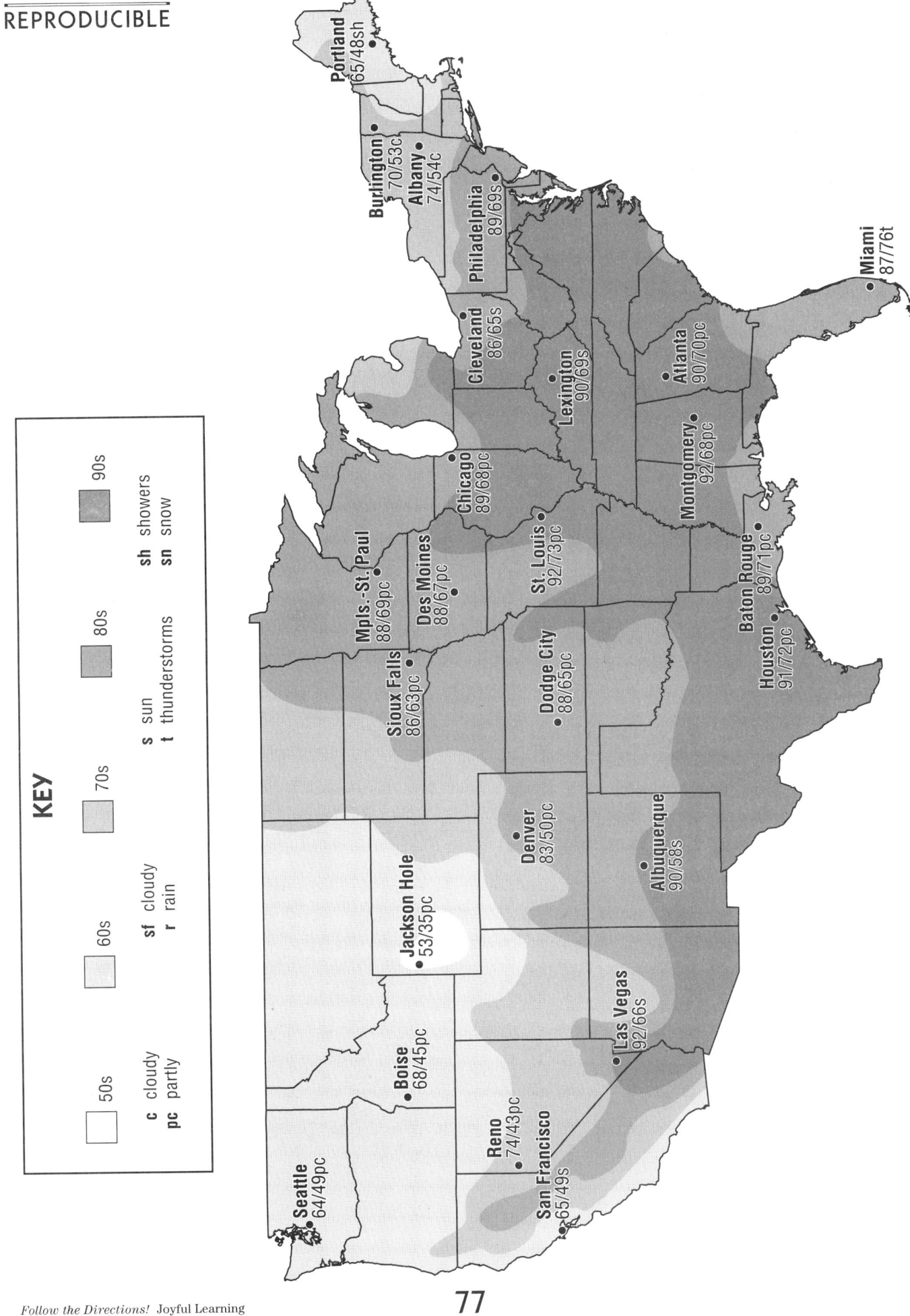

KEY

☐ 50s	☐ 60s	☐ 70s
☐ 80s	☐ 90s	

- **c** cloudy
- **pc** partly cloudy
- **sf** cloudy
- **r** rain
- **s** sun
- **t** thunderstorms
- **sh** showers
- **sn** snow

Portland 65/48sh
Burlington 70/53c
Albany 74/54c
Philadelphia 89/69s
Miami 87/76t
Cleveland 86/65s
Lexington 90/69s
Atlanta 90/70pc
Montgomery 92/68pc
Chicago 89/68pc
Mpls.-St. Paul 88/69pc
Des Moines 88/67pc
St. Louis 92/73pc
Baton Rouge 89/71pc
Sioux Falls 86/63pc
Dodge City 88/65pc
Houston 91/72pc
Denver 83/50pc
Albuquerque 90/58s
Jackson Hole 53/35pc
Las Vegas 92/66s
Boise 68/45pc
Reno 74/43pc
San Francisco 65/49s
Seattle 64/49pc

Follow the Directions! Joyful Learning

77

flood ▶ fluid

flood (fluhd) *verb*
1. When something, such as a river, **floods**, it overflows with water beyond its normal limits.
2. To overwhelm, or to come in large amounts. *The charity was flooded with offers of help.*
▷ *verb* **flooding, flooded** ▷ *noun* **flood**

flood·light (fluhd-*lite*) *noun* A lamp that produces a broad and very bright beam of light.

flood plain *noun* An area of low land near a stream or river that becomes flooded during heavy rains.

floor (flor)
1. *noun* The flat surface that you walk or stand on inside a building. ▷ *noun* **flooring**
2. *noun* A story in a building. *The skyscraper has over 40 floors.*
3. *verb* (*informal*) To surprise. *Maria was floored by the news.* ▷ **flooring, floored**

flop (flop) *verb*
1. To fall or drop heavily. *Sarah flopped into a chair.*
2. To flap or move about. *The kite flopped about in the breeze.* ▷ *adjective* **floppy**
3. (*informal*) To fail. *The play flopped.* ▷ *noun* **flop**
▷ *verb* **flopping, flopped**

floppy disk *noun* A small, thin piece of flexible plastic coated with magnetic particles used for storing information from a computer. See **computer**.

flo·ra (flor-uh) *noun* The plant life of a particular area, as in *desert flora*.

flo·ral (flor-uhl) *adjective* Of, relating to, or showing flowers, as in *a floral arrangement* or *floral curtains*.

flo·rist (flor-ist) *noun* Someone who sells flowers and plants.

floss (flawss *or* floss) *noun* A thin strand of thread used to clean between the teeth. Also called *dental floss*.

flot·sam (flot-suhm) *noun* Objects from a shipwreck that float in the sea or are washed up on the shore.

floun·der (floun-dur)
1. *verb* To struggle through water, snow, mud, etc.
2. *verb* To have difficulties coping with something. *Bill is floundering with his science project.*
3. *noun* A flat ocean fish used for food.
▷ *verb* **floundering, floundered**

flour (flou-ur) *noun* Ground wheat or other grain that you use for baking. **Flour** sounds like **flower**.
▷ *adjective* **floury**

flour·ish (flur-ish) *verb*
1. To grow and succeed. *Our garden flourished.*
2. To wave something around in order to show it off. *Jan flourished her medal.* ▷ *noun* **flourish**
▷ *verb* **flourishes, flourishing, flourished**

flout (flout) *verb* If you **flout** the rules, you break them deliberately. ▷ **flouting, flouted**

flow (floh) *verb* To move along smoothly, like a river. ▷ **flowing, flowed** ▷ *noun* **flow**

flow·chart (floh-*chart*) *noun* A diagram that shows how something develops and progresses, step by step.

flow·er (flou-ur)
1. *noun* The colored part of a plant that produces seeds or fruit.
2. *verb* To produce flowers. ▷ **flowering, flowered**
3. *noun* A plant that has flowers.
Flour sounds like **flower**.

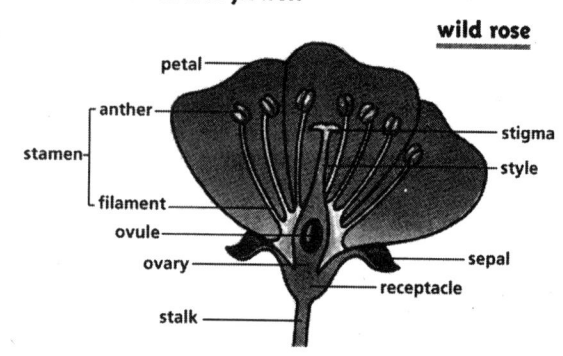

wild rose

petal, anther, stamen, filament, ovule, ovary, stalk, stigma, style, sepal, receptacle

flu (floo) *noun* An illness that is like a bad cold, with fever and muscle pains. Flu is short for *influenza*. It is caused by a virus.

fluc·tu·ate (fluhk-choo-ate) *verb* To change back and forth or up and down. *Gasoline prices keep fluctuating.* ▷ **fluctuating, fluctuated** ▷ *noun* **fluctuation**

flue (floo) *noun* A hollow part or passage, such as the pipe inside a chimney that carries smoke away from a fire. See **termite**.

flu·ent (floo-uhnt) *adjective* Able to speak smoothly and clearly, especially in another language. *John is fluent in French.* ▷ *noun* **fluency** ▷ *adverb* **fluently**

fluff (fluhf)
1. *noun* A light, soft, downy substance.
2. *verb* When a bird **fluffs** its feathers, it shakes them out.
3. *verb* To make a mistake in speaking or reading something. *He fluffed his lines in the play.*
▷ *verb* **fluffing, fluffed**

fluff·y (fluhf-ee) *adjective*
1. Light and airy, as in *a fluffy pillow*.
2. Covered with soft, fine hair or feathers, as in *a fluffy rabbit*.
▷ *adjective* **fluffier, fluffiest**

flu·id (floo-id)
1. *noun* A flowing substance, either a liquid or a gas. *Water, oil, and nitrogen are fluids.*
2. *adjective* Flowing, or liquid. ▷ *noun* **fluidity**

tenuous ▶ terrarium

ten·u·ous (ten-yoo-uhss) *adjective* Not very strong or substantial; shaky. *He had a tenuous grasp of the test material.* ▷ *adverb* **tenuously**

te·pee (tee-pee) *noun* A tent shaped like a cone and made from animal skins by North American Indians.

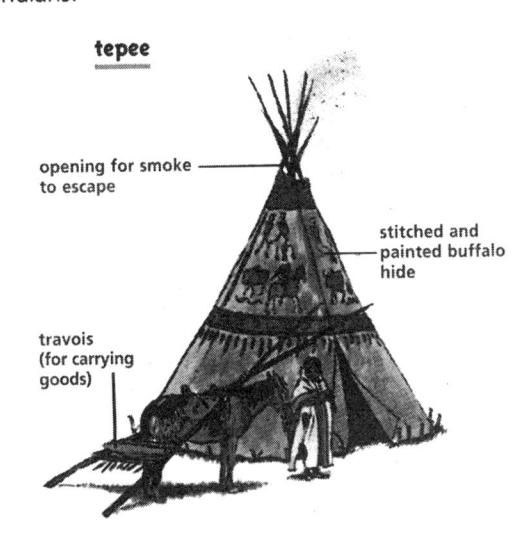

tepee
- opening for smoke to escape
- stitched and painted buffalo hide
- travois (for carrying goods)

tep·id (tep-id) *adjective* Slightly warm; lukewarm.

ter·i·ya·ki (ter-ee-yah-kee) *noun* A Japanese dish of chicken, meat, or fish that has been soaked in soy sauce and broiled or grilled.

term (turm) *noun*
1. A word with a specific meaning in some particular field, as in *musical terms* or *computer terms*.
2. A definite or limited period of time. *A president's term of office is four years.*
3. A part of the school year.
4. **terms** *noun, plural* The conditions of an agreement, a contract, a will, or a sale.
5. **terms** *noun, plural* A relationship between people. *After the argument, we were on good terms again.*

ter·mi·nal (tur-muh-nuhl)
1. *noun* A station at either end of a transportation line, as in *an airport terminal*.
2. *noun* A computer keyboard and screen linked to a network.
3. *adjective* If someone has a **terminal** illness, he or she cannot be cured and will die from it.
4. **Terminal velocity** is the maximum speed an object can reach falling through the air.
▷ *adverb* **terminally**

ter·mi·nate (tur-muh-nate) *verb* To stop or to end. *The train terminates here. We decided to terminate our agreement.* ▷ **terminating, terminated**

ter·mite (tur-mite) *noun* An antlike insect that eats wood. Termites build large mounds, where they live together in colonies. *The picture shows the inside of a termite mound.*

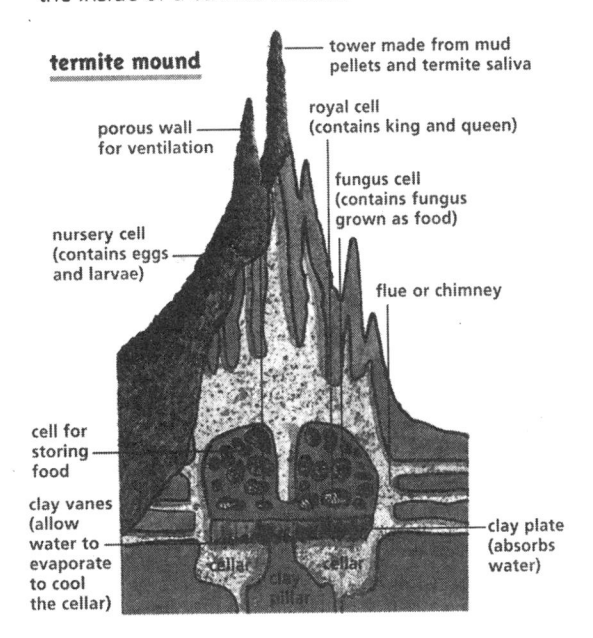

termite mound
- tower made from mud pellets and termite saliva
- porous wall for ventilation
- royal cell (contains king and queen)
- fungus cell (contains fungus grown as food)
- nursery cell (contains eggs and larvae)
- flue or chimney
- cell for storing food
- clay vanes (allow water to evaporate to cool the cellar)
- clay plate (absorbs water)

ter·race (ter-iss) *noun*
1. A paved, open area next to a house; a patio.
2. A balcony of an apartment building.
3. A raised, flat platform of land with sloping sides.
▷ *adjective* **terraced**

ter·ra-cot·ta (ter-uh kot-uh) *noun* A hard, waterproof clay used in making pottery and roofs. ▷ *adjective* **terra-cotta**

ter·rain (tuh-rayn) *noun* Ground, or land. *The terrain was very rocky.*

ter·ra·pin (ter-uh-pin) *noun* A North American turtle that lives in or near fresh water or along seashores. *The picture shows a diamondback terrapin from the East Coast of the United States. The diamondback gets its name from the shapes on its shell.*

terrapin

ter·rar·i·um (tuh-rer-ee-uhm) *noun* A glass or plastic container for growing small plants or raising small land animals. ▷ *noun, plural* **terrariums** *or* **terraria** (tuh-rer-ee-uh)

555

Pie Chart